A Beginner's Guide to WordStar,® 1-2-3,® and dBASE®

For Computers Using PC-DOS or MS-DOS

Charles S. Parker

The College of Santa Fe
Santa Fe, New Mexico

The Colorado College
Colorado Springs, Colorado

Holt, Rinehart and Winston

New York Chicago San Francisco Philadelphia
Montreal Toronto London Sydney Tokyo
Mexico City Rio de Janeiro Madrid

dBASE, dBASE II, dBASE III, and dBASE III Plus are trademarks of Ashton-Tate.
WordStar, MailMerge, and SpellStar are trademarks of Micropro International Corporation.
1-2-3 and Symphony are trademarks of Lotus Development Corporation.
IBM PC, IBM PC XT, IBM PC AT, and PC DOS are trademarks of International Business Machines Corporation.
MS-DOS is a trademark of Microsoft Corporation.
KnowledgeMan is a trademark of Micro Data Base Systems, Inc.
TI Professional Computer is a tradename of Texas Instruments, Inc.
AT&T 6300 PC is a trademark of AT&T.
Tandy 1000 is a tradename of Radio Shack, A Division of Tandy Corporation.
Zenith Z-150 is a trademark of Zenith Data Systems.
Leading Edge PC is a trademark of Leading Edge Products, Inc.
Compaq Portable and Compaq Deskpro (Model 2) are trademarks of COMPAQ Computer Corporation.

Address correspondence to:
383 Madison Avenue, New York, NY 10017

ISBN 0-03-013018-2

Printed in the United States of America

Published simultaneously in Canada
7 8 9 0 066 9 8 7 6 5 4 3 2

CBS COLLEGE PUBLISHING
Holt, Rinehart and Winston
The Dryden Press
Saunders College Publishing

Contents

Preface

One of the most welcome changes in computing during the past several years has been the arrival of *productivity software packages* such as word processors, spreadsheets, and database management systems. These software products have gotten their names because they can increase the on-the-job productivity of nearly anyone who has access to a computer system. Not too long ago, it virtually took a degree in some computer-related field to be able to work directly with computers and the software that controlled them. Today, through the availability of inexpensive desktop microcomputer systems and easy-to-use productivity software, any business person—from clerical worker to company president—can effectively tap the power of computers.

A Beginner's Guide to WordStar, 1-2-3, and dBASE—which is to be used as a companion text to *Understanding Computers and Data Processing: Today and Tomorrow,* Second Edition—discusses the basics of three widely used productivity software products: WordStar (a word processor), 1-2-3 (a spreadsheet package with several support functions integrated into it), and dBASE II and III (two database management systems). These packages, which each have the largest user bases in their respective markets, are proprietary. That is, they are each the property of some software vendor and can only be legally operated if an appropriate use license has been acquired from the vendor. Although these software products (and many similar ones) are not free, fortunately they are inexpensive enough to be within the budgets of most users who need them in their work. When you think about it, a $300 package that may save thousands of dollars in typing, filing, or budget-preparation costs is a real bargain.

The first two sections of the *Guide* include some background information relating to using your microcomputer system. Before we get started, keep in mind that you'll have to put in a lot of hard work if you want to fully take advantage of the power that productivity software puts at your fingertips. Although you can learn to do things such as word process a simple letter in an hour or so, it often takes several weeks of practice to use a word processor effectively as a tool for preparing polished, typeset-quality manuscripts. And although you may bumble successfully through your first spreadsheet exercises in a morning or afternoon, it will take considerably more time with spreadsheet software to be able to use it in clever ways that can mean thousands of dollars in labor savings on your job.

Users of this *Guide* are assumed to be working on computer systems with either the PC-DOS or MS-DOS operating systems. The computer system should be equipped with at least 256 kilobytes of main memory (less memory is required if only WordStar is used) and two floppy disk drives.

Charles S. Parker

Section 1

Read Me First: An Introduction

Here you are. First day in the computer lab. Grasped in one hand is a WordStar, 1-2-3, or dBASE program disk that you want to learn to use. In the other hand is a blank floppy disk that will eventually contain the work you do when using one of these programs. Squarely in front of you, a computer system that you must contend with. What to do next?

Relax. If you systematically organize a few notions in your mind before you even touch your computer, every action that you subsequently take won't seem quite so mysterious. For example, think for a moment how strange it would be operating a car for the first time if you never saw a car or a road, and you really didn't understand what purpose cars and roads served. If your driving instructor just said, "Turn the key and put your foot on the accelerator," you'd probably be very nervous. So don't subject yourself to the same sort of torture when learning how to use computers. Sometimes it's better to take a few minutes to learn about the "forest" before you become intimidated by the "trees."

This *Guide* is organized in an easy-to-follow fashion. The discussion of each package begins with what the package is designed to do. Following this is an overview of how the package works—a discussion of the "big picture" (so you can distinguish the forest from the trees later on when you wade through the operational details of the package). Next is a simple, graduated set of examples that will instruct you on the package fundamentals—what you should know about things such as invoking the package from your computer's operating system, executing a few fundamental operations, saving your work, and returning to the operating system. Finally, you'll learn a variety of other useful commands.

Whatever your current level of computer expertise, you should read over Sections 1 and 2 of the *Guide* before you start. If you know very little about computers, read the next subsection especially carefully.

SOME THINGS YOU SHOULD KNOW IF YOU'RE RELATIVELY UNFAMILIAR WITH COMPUTERS

It's impossible to provide a complete course in computers in just a few pages. So, what we'll do here is touch briefly on some very fundamental concepts—those you must be familiar with just to get started. Whenever you want to gain a deeper understanding of these concepts, refer to the recommended coverage in *Understanding Computers and Data Processing* where appropriate.

Hardware, Software, and Files

First of all, let's consider the computer system components you'll be interacting with: hardware, software, and files.

Hardware refers to the equipment on which you'll be working. Your computer unit (or system unit), keyboard, monitor, floppy disk unit, and printer are examples of hardware. Shortly we'll be discussing what you should know about each of these pieces of equipment.

Software refers to computer programs. The *Guide* discusses three applications software products—WordStar, 1-2-3, and dBASE. We refer to them as *applications software* because they tell the computer how to perform a specific, job-related task (application), such as preparing letters or maintaining employee records. Here, the terms productivity software and applications software will be used interchangeably. It's likely that the applications software packages you'll be working with are encoded on floppy disks. These software disks are commonly called *program disks.*

There is also another type of software—*systems software.* You must interact with systems software to gain access to WordStar, 1-2-3, dBASE, or any other applications software. The piece of systems software that you'll be most concerned with here is your *operating system,* which is named either PC-DOS or MS-DOS. Learning to use your operating system effectively is just as important as learning how to use any applications software package. It enables you to do things such as prepare new disks for use on your computer system, copy the full or partial contents of one disk onto another disk, and determine what is on your disk.

The term *files* refers to the material you'll be creating with applications software. With a word processor the files you create are such things as letters, manuscripts, and book chapters; with spreadsheet software, budgets, asset amortization tables, and profit-and-loss statements; with database management systems, a group of employee records, vendor records, and client records. Generally, you'll be storing these files on the blank floppy disk you purchased or were given. In Section 2, you will learn how to format this disk, thereby making it usable on your computer system.

In a two-disk-drive system most people reserve the "first" (leftmost or topmost) disk drive for the program disk and the "second" (rightmost or bottommost) disk drive for the disk to contain the data files. This convention should be followed rigorously if you wish to avoid clumsy mistakes. The first and second drives are commonly referred to as the *A drive* and *B drive* respectively. Also, many users cover the *write-protection-notch* (see *Understanding Computers and Data Processing,* pages 136 and 138) on their program disks to ensure they don't accidentally destroy the programs on them.

Primary and Secondary Memory

The computer system you'll be using employs electronic *memory* to store both data and programs. If you are a beginner to computers, you must learn the differences between your system's primary memory and secondary memory.

Physically, *primary memory* (often referred to as *main memory*—or sometimes *RAM*, for *random-access memory*)—pertains to the storage chips that are mounted onto boards inside your computer's system unit, while *secondary memory* usually refers to disk storage. The conceptual difference between the two is that primary memory is temporary and stores only what the computer system is currently working on while its power is up. Secondary memory, on the other hand, is semi-permanent. It doesn't change unless you specifically summon the computer system to "write" (save) something onto it. The computer system itself generally controls the contents of primary memory whereas you control the contents of secondary memory.

When your computer's power is shut off, the contents of primary memory will be lost, but what you have stored on disk won't be erased. Later you'll learn how to save files on disk and how to retrieve them. Both saving and retrieving can be done through either an applications software command or an operating system command. One of the most frustrating experiences for any newcomer to computers is turning off the computer's power (thereby erasing the contents of RAM) before an important file has been saved onto disk. Once you have saved something onto disk, it is an easy matter to load it back into primary memory again.

Primary and secondary memory capacities on your computer system are measured in *bytes*. Roughly speaking, a byte is equivalent to a single character of data. So, for example, a 300-character memo prepared on WordStar occupies roughly 300 bytes of storage space. Often memory capacities are stated in thousands of bytes, or *kilobytes* (KB). Two common capacities are 256 KB RAM in the computer's system unit and 360 KB for floppy disks.

LEARNING PRODUCTIVITY SOFTWARE: SOME TIPS

Often before you learn anything new, you'll look to others for some general advice on how to proceed. Below are four tips that you may find helpful when learning to use productivity software.

A Few Commands Go a Long Way

Instead of trying at the outset to learn as many commands as you can possibly pick up, first try mastering the few commands you'll need to do the exercises at hand. You can pick up others later as you encounter problems that necessitate using them.

For example, with WordStar, you'll first be creating small documents, so that your keyboard's arrow keys will be sufficient to move around through the text (a character at a time). However, as your documents get longer, you'll need to move through text faster. This will necessitate learning to use special keys and commands that will send you through large blocks of text at a time. Software designers generally try to make their products easy to use. If you find yourself doing something that seems very labor-intensive, that's when it's time to look around for a more powerful command.

Oddly enough you'll find that mastering just 15% or so of the available commands in any package will probably enable you to do 85% or so of the work you'll ever need or want to do with the package.

Resources

Say you do want to learn a more powerful command and you can't find it in this *Guide*. Where do you go? Fortunately, there is a rich variety of resources available on WordStar, 1-2-3, and dBASE to enable you to go well beyond what you learn here. The popularity of these packages ensures that a wide assortment of instructional materials will be present in the marketplace. Five useful types of resources are disk tutorials, video cassettes, training manuals, trade books, and reference manuals.

Several disk tutorials are available for each of the productivity software packages covered in this *Guide*. To use one of these instructional disks you put the disk into a disk drive (usually the A drive), invoke the tutorial through a special command, and follow the instructions that will subsequently appear on the screen. Generally the disks tell you which keys to press and explain to you the resulting output from each key sequence. Tutorial disks are available through both productivity software vendors and "third-party" training companies (such as American Training International in Manhattan Beach, California and Cdex Corporation in Los Altos, California).

Both training manuals and instructional video cassettes are like tutorial disks in that they are step-by-step learning tools. As with tutorial disks, many third-party companies produce training manuals and video cassettes for popular productivity software packages. The quality of some of these third-party products can be exceptional, since the companies producing them live or die on how well they are able to train people.

There is a wealth of trade books available on WordStar, 1-2-3, and dBASE. These books can be quite useful because they may go through a very large and comprehensive set of examples to make you familiar with a package. Also, they may cover extensively a particular aspect of a package that you want to learn about in some depth. Since there are so many trade books now available, there is a good chance that you'll find one written at a level that meshes well with your level of understanding. Your best bet in locating such books is to wander down to the computer section of your local bookstore and browse. Also, some college and university libraries stock such books along with their other holdings.

USING PRODUCTIVITY SOFTWARE: BASIC OPERATIONS

- *Accessing* the package from the operation system.
- Informing the package that you either want to *create* a new file or *retrieve* an old one from disk.
- Commanding the package to *save* a file onto disk.
- Commanding the package to *print* a file.
- Commanding the package to *delete* a file that's on disk.
- Indicating to the package that you want to *quit* working on your current file and do something on another file.
- *Leaving* the package and returning to the operating system.

Figure 1-1. Fundamental productivity software operations.

When all else fails in your search for an answer, you must often resort to the comprehensive reference manual provided by the vendor of your software package. Vendor reference manuals generally are written on a more technical level than trade books, but they are the final word on what a package can and can't do. If the reference manual fails you, call up a knowledgeable friend or the software vendor.

Experiment Freely

A joke sometimes told about high-level business executives is that they tinker first and (if not successful) read the instructions later. This technique can actually be extremely helpful when learning how to use a productivity software package. These packages often beckon you to do things that require you to use your intuition. Using your intuition will often produce faster results than looking something up and reading several paragraphs. If you're unsure about how to proceed beyond a certain point, and the cost of making a mistake isn't high, try something that seems reasonable. People who wait until they're absolutely certain about how to proceed before taking any action just won't learn these packages very fast.

Packages Have the Same Fundamental Operations

Finally, you should observe that most productivity software packages have in common seven basic operations. These are shown in Figure 1-1. In the *Guide* these operations will generally be the first ones you learn as you study WordStar, 1-2-3, or dBASE. Depending on the package you use, the file that you work on may be a word-processed *document*, a *spreadsheet*, or a *set of records*.

Section 2

The Operating Environment

Before you dive right into working with an applications software package, it helps to know something about the operating environment in which these packages work. Although there are a great number of subjects that we could discuss about this environment, we'll examine only two here: the support hardware available with your microcomputer and the PC-DOS and MS-DOS operating systems.

SUPPORT HARDWARE

Most likely, the hardware configuration you'll be working on includes the following items:

- A system unit
- A monitor
- A printer
- A keyboard
- Two floppy disk drives (which may be built into your system unit)

These devices are shown in Figure 2-1. We'll now discuss each of them.

The System Unit

Your microcomputer's *system unit* was described in some depth in Chapter 4 of *Understanding Computers and Data Processing,* pages 111–118. This device is the "box" that contains the system board (with your microprocessor and main memory) as well as a variety of related circuitry.

When you're working with any productivity software package the single most important operational detail you should know about the system unit is the location of the power switch. The system unit (and monitor and printer, as well) has a switch that turns its power on and off. You'll either have to turn on your system unit, monitor, and printer individually or, if your computer system has a *power manager* that controls all of these devices, you can flick one switch to turn them all on or off together. Remember, the system unit contains the computer's primary memory, so when you turn the system unit off, the contents of this memory are erased.

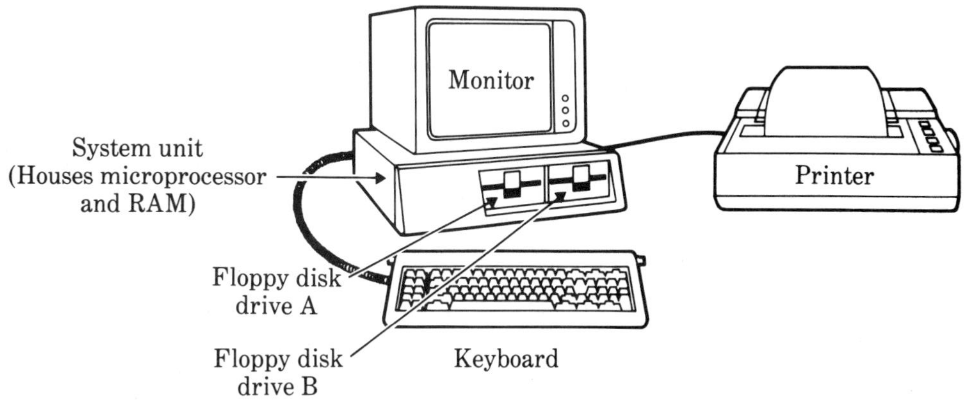

Figure 2-1. A typical microcomputer system.

The Monitor

Monitors resemble TV sets (see Chapter 6 of *Understanding Computers and Data Processing*). Besides having a power switch, most monitors have contrast and brightness knobs that enable you to adjust the image of the screen to suit your visual preferences. Monitor screens are either *monochrome* (one foreground color) or *full-color* (eight or more colors).

The Printer

In recent years *printers* available for microcomputer systems have improved dramatically. There are so many variations among printers (see Chapter 6 in *Understanding Computers and Data Processing*) that it is impossible to catalog all of them here.

Most likely you will be working on a low-speed, *impact dot-matrix printer*. Many of these have features to provide an assortment of print typefaces—including both draft-quality and near-letter-quality (NLQ) print, boldfacing, subscripts and superscripts, compressed characters, elongated characters, graphical characters, and so on. If you are interested in exploring the features of your printer further, consult the operations manual available from its vendor.

The Keyboard

The *keyboard* of your microcomputer system is an extremely powerful device. Most keyboards are controlled by specialized computer chips. Chances are the keyboard you'll be working with looks something like the one in Figure 2-2. This is the keyboard available with the IBM PC. On many keyboards the keys are *typematic;* that is, they repeat as long as you hold them down.

Many keyboards have three sections. In the center is the *typewriter section*. The arrangement of the keys is similar to that on a conventional typewriter. There are, however, many special keys that you may not have

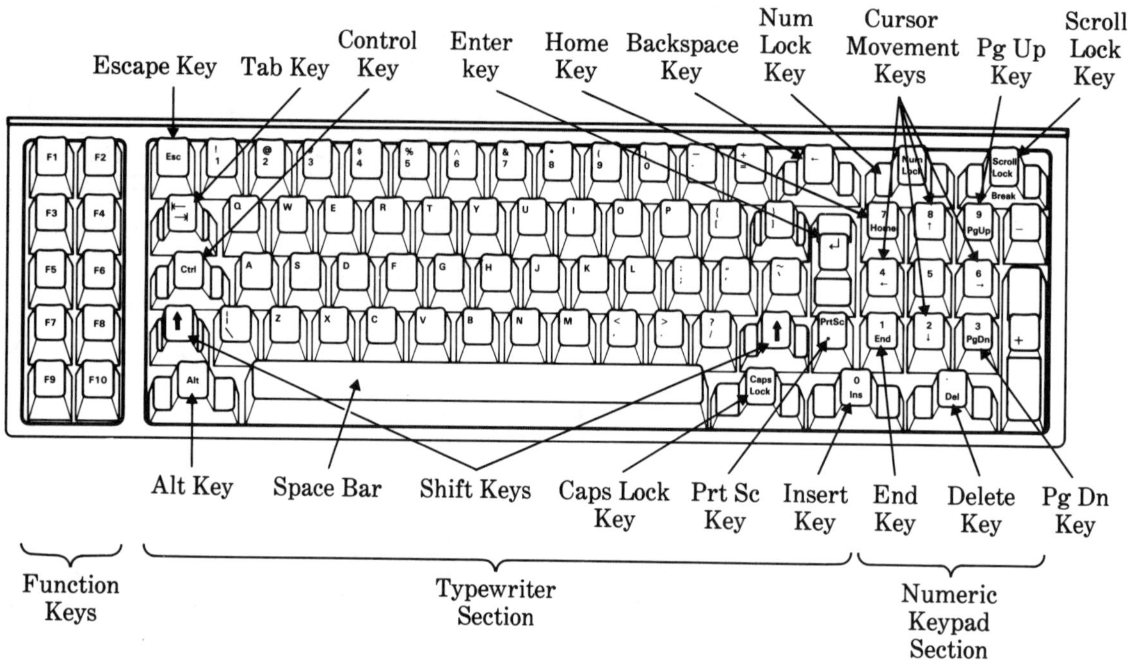

Figure 2-2. The IBM PC keyboard.

encountered before, such as the Alt, Esc, and PrtSc keys. We'll discuss these and other special keys shortly. One thing you should know right now, however, is that every productivity software package uses these special keys in its own way. For example, the Del key works completely differently in WordStar than it does in dBASE.

On the keyboard that accompanies the IBM PC, to the left of the typewriter section are the *function keys.* These, too, are special keys and each of them has a different meaning in each software package. For example, if you are using WordStar on the IBM PC, the F2 key is used to block-indent paragraphs. In 1-2-3, the F2 key is used to switch into the edit mode.

Not all keyboards have 10 function keys as does the IBM PC. Also, these keys may be positioned differently than they are on the IBM PC's keyboard and may even have different meanings for the same software package. For example, the keyboard available with the TI Professional Computer has 12 function keys, located at the top of the typewriter section rather than to the left of it. What's more, if you use WordStar on your "TI Pro," the F2 key will reformat paragraphs, not block-indent them as on the IBM PC.

In spite of these differences, function keys are really easy to use and tremendously helpful. Each of them is designed to perform an operation on a single keystroke, saving you keying time. In many applications software packages, the operations performed by the function keys are shown at the bottom of your monitor screen.

The *numeric keypad section* is a cluster of number keys and special keys. On most keyboards it is located to the right of the typewriter section. The numeric keypad is handy to use if you are trained—as are many people—to enter numbers from a cluster of keys arranged in this configuration.

As we discuss each software package we'll be mentioning the significance of several of these special keys. There are, however, a number of important keys and keystroke sequences that you should be familiar with right away. These are:

Enter Key

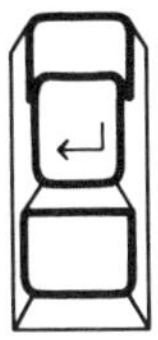

The **Enter** (or **Return**) key is used to enter commands to the computer system in whatever software package you'll be using. In many cases, before this key is depressed, everything you type is held in a special memory area called an *input buffer,* awaiting corrections, before being sent on.

Arrow Keys

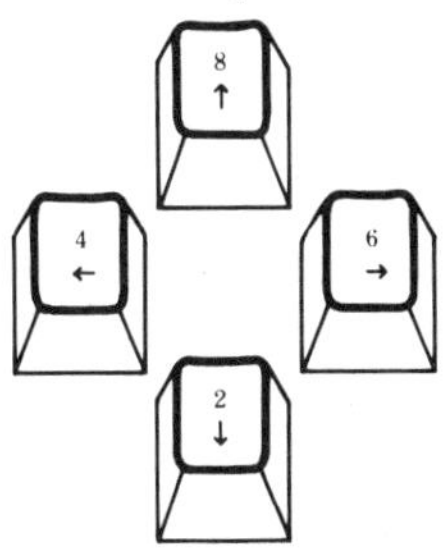

The four **arrow keys** are used to move some pointer—such as a cursor or highlight—around the screen. In 1-2-3 these keys can also be used effectively at certain times to enter data.

Escape Key

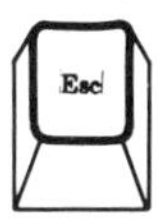

The **Escape** key is commonly used to abort some action that you've previously taken at the keyboard. In 1-2-3 you can also use this key to backtrack to some previous point in a command sequence.

Delete Key

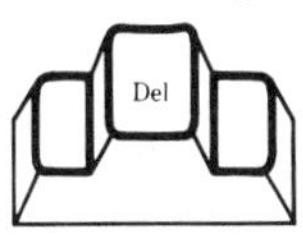

The **Delete** key enables you to remove characters. In 1-2-3 and dBASE this key removes characters at the cursor position. In WordStar it removes characters to the left of the cursor position.

Insert Key

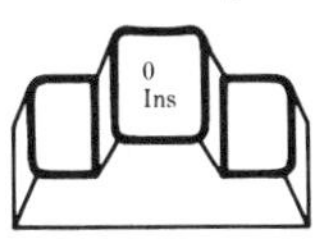

The **Insert** key allows you to insert characters. In WordStar and dBASE, this key enables you to insert characters at the cursor position. Also, it works as a *toggle key,* that is, it activates a command (insertion) when you depress it once and deactivates the command when you depress it again. In 1-2-3 the Insert key is inactive.

Backspace Key

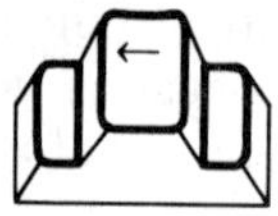

The **Backspace** key moves the cursor back one space. In 1-2-3 and dBASE, this key will also erase characters as it backspaces to their positions. In WordStar this key erases characters when you are naming files but not when you are editing documents.

NumLock Key

The **NumLock** key is used to activate the numeric keypad section of the keyboard. This key also can be an annoyance because it can easily be hit by mistake and deactivate the arrow keys. So, if depressing the arrow keys produces numbers on your screen, hit the NumLock key again (it's also a toggle key) to deactivate the numeric keypad.

CapsLock Key

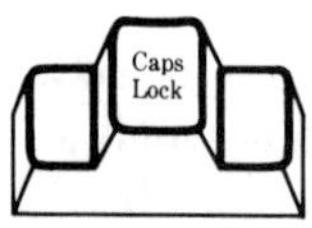

The **CapsLock** key is used to produce uppercase letters on your keyboard, saving you from having to depress the shift key. This key can be very handy when typing titles that consist only of uppercase letters. CapsLock is also a toggle key, so you can deactivate it by hitting it again.

Ctrl-Alt-Delete
Key Sequence

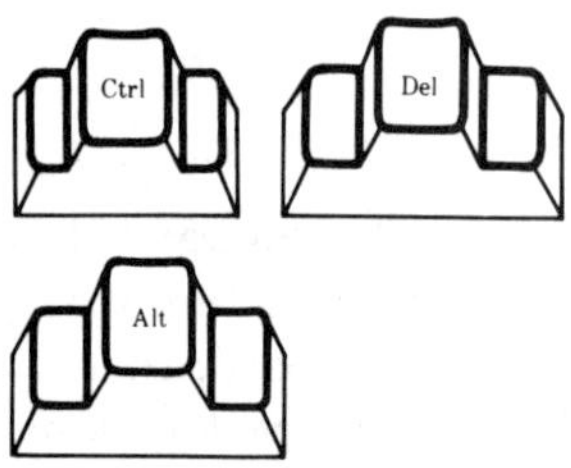

If you hold down the **Ctrl** and **Alt** keys (which work like shift keys) and then hit the **Delete** key, the sequence will cause a *warm boot* of your computer system. This is virtually equivalent to turning your computer off and then on again. Probably everyone working on a microcomputer system has faced some situation where proceeding with an applications software package was not possible, necessitating this drastic action. If you execute this key sequence, everything you currently have saved in main memory will be lost.

Shift-PrtSc
Key Sequence

The **Shift-PrtSc** sequence of keys enables you to send whatever is currently on your monitor screen to the printer. If what you want to send to the printer can fit onto a single screen, and you're not overly concerned about getting some extraneous characters that you see on the screen on your output, this is the best (and the fastest) way to get output. Using this sequence of keys provides an excellent way to copy a file or error message from the display screen, so that you can later discuss it with your instructor.

The Disk Drives

Many *floppy disk drives,* such as the ones in Figure 2-1, are built into their system units. Many system units contain two disk drives and, as already mentioned, these are referred to as the A and B drives. The computer system can only be "pointing" to one of these drives at any time for reading or writing. The drive that the computer system is currently pointing to is called the *logged drive* or *default drive.* The next subsections, on DOS, discuss the disk operations and file-naming procedures you must know when working on your computer system.

Inserting a disk into a floppy disk unit and caring for *floppy disks* was covered in Chapter 5 of *Understanding Computers and Data Processing,* pages 138–141. If you've never worked on a floppy disk system before, you should carefully read these text pages. Four things you absolutely need to know are:

- The disk unit will only work if the disk is installed properly in the drive.
- You should never attempt to remove or install a disk in a drive when that drive's *indicator light* is on.
- Never touch the surface of the disk that is exposed in the disk's *recording window.* Like the phonograph records or musical tapes you have at home, floppy disks should be treated with respect.
- You cannot write to your 5¼-inch floppy disk if the disk's *write-protect notch* is covered.

THE PC-DOS AND MS-DOS OPERATING SYSTEMS

The operating system is your gateway to all of the applications programs on your computer system. It also manages your disk files, enabling you to save, retrieve, copy, and erase them. You work with your operating system—either PC-DOS or MS-DOS—by issuing DOS commands (see the next subsection). *DOS,* incidentally, stands for *D*isk *O*perating *S*ystem.

Both PC-DOS and MS-DOS were developed by Microsoft Corporation, of Bellevue, Washington. Except for a few minor differences, these operating systems are virtually identical. PC-DOS was created originally for the IBM PC, while MS-DOS was devised to operate on computers that look and work a lot like the IBM PC. A few examples of such computers are the TI Professional Computer, Leading Edge PC, Compaq Deskpro (Model 2), Compaq Portable, AT&T 6300 PC, Tandy 1000, and Zenith Z-150.

Both the PC-DOS and MS-DOS operating systems have been revised many times since they first were developed. Each major revision is referred to as a *version* (sometimes also called a *revision* or *release*). All versions starting with the number 1 (such as 1.0 and 1.1) were designed for the earliest 16-bit microcomputer systems, which used only floppy disks and cassette tapes for secondary storage. In late 1983, when IBM came out with its PC XT computer, a machine that featured a built-in hard disk, version 2.0 of DOS was developed to deal with the intricacies associated with storing data on a large-capacity secondary storage device. Improved revisions of this "hard disk version" of DOS (such as 2.1, 2.2, and 2.3) followed. Later, in 1984, when IBM announced its multiuser IBM PC AT computer, an entirely new set of DOS versions (such as 3.0 and 3.1) followed.

All of these versions of DOS are "upward compatible." What this means is that later versions of DOS can work with both applications programs and data files that were created on earlier versions. Whichever version of DOS you use, it will probably be contained on a floppy disk, which is commonly referred to as the "DOS disk" or "system disk."

To start your computer system and work with DOS, place your DOS disk in the A drive of your computer's system unit, close the drive door, and turn on your system unit (as well as your monitor). You'll now hear some noise taking place inside the system unit before the first message is displayed on your monitor screen. What is happening here is that you are *booting up* your system. What takes place during the booting-up process is that certain operating system commands are read into main memory, so that the computer can access them quickly.

The commands that the operating system boots into its main memory are called *internal commands.* You can issue these commands at any time your computer system is on, no matter what disks are present in the drives. The commands that are not stored in internal memory when the system is booted up are called *external commands.* For you to issue these commands, the DOS disk must be present in one of the drives. By convention the A drive is used, since DOS, too, is a program.

Once your system is booted up, you'll see a message indicating the version of DOS you are using, followed by a prompt asking you to enter the date. If, for example, the date is February 1, 1987 you would enter this date as follows:

2-1-87 (cr)

where (cr)—for carriage return—represents depressing the Enter key.

DOS is particular about how you enter the date, and you have to enter it in the form shown. When you enter the date in this way, DOS will record it on your disk's file directory when you save files. If you don't wish to enter a date, hit the Enter key, and DOS will proceed to prompt you for the time.

The time is entered in a similar manner. Time is expressed in hours:minutes:seconds.hundredths. Hours can be between 0 and 23; minutes and seconds between 0 and 59. Most people omit the hundredths entry and, often, the seconds entry. So, for example, if it is 10:35 A.M. you enter the time as

10:35 (cr)

Or, if it is 6:23 P.M., you would enter

18:23 (cr)

If you don't wish to enter a time, hit the Enter key to proceed.

The next prompt that you will encounter is DOS's A-drive command prompt, which is either

A> or A:

depending on which version of DOS you are using. What DOS is telling you here is that it has finished with its signing-in procedure and it's ready for your first DOS command.

Any time this prompt appears you can enter one of a variety of DOS commands. A description of some of the most important of these follows in the next subsection. Some of these commands explicitly name one or more files on which you want DOS to operate. In the final subsection of this section, we'll be discussing rules for naming DOS files.

SOME USEFUL DOS COMMANDS

Each of the commands that follows must be issued after DOS has provided you with a command prompt; for example A> or B> (or A: or B:). For clarity, both DOS's command prompt and the keystrokes you enter (shown in a boldface font) are shown. After you type in a command you must hit the Enter key, which is indicated by

(cr)

To learn about DOS commands not covered in the *Guide,* consult a DOS reference manual or a trade book devoted to DOS.

Formatting a Disk

The FORMAT command enables you to prepare a disk for use on your computer. Formatting is an important operation because every "fresh" disk you buy must be formatted on your machine before you can store anything on it. You can also use the FORMAT command on one of your "old" disks that has already been formatted one or more times. The FORMAT command will erase all files currently on the disk.

Generally, you'll format disks using the following procedure. Place your DOS disk in the A drive and the disk to be formatted in the B drive. At DOS's A> prompt, issue the FORMAT command as follows:

A>**FORMAT B: (cr)**

A message will next appear asking you to strike any key if you are ready. Since you are, strike a key. At this point, your computer system will be tied up for several seconds while your disk is being formatted in the B drive.

When the formatting is finished, DOS will apprise you of its success in formatting the disk. If the format was totally successful you should get a message such as

Formatting . . . Format complete

362496 bytes total disk space
362496 bytes available on disk

Format another? (Y/N)_

Hit the **N** key at this time if you don't want to format another disk.

Sometimes formatting will not go so well and you'll be notified that there are some bad tracks on your disk that couldn't be formatted. If this is the case, you can try to manage with the bad tracks or try formatting your disk on another computer. Disk drives frequently get out of alignment, and it is more likely that the formatting problem is due to the disk drive, not the disk.

FORMAT is an external command, so your DOS disk must be present in the A drive when you issue this command.

Calling for a Disk Directory

The DIR command produces a display of the names of the files that are stored on a disk in one of the drives. For example, if you are logged onto drive A, issue

A>**DIR (cr)**

to get a listing of filenames on the A drive. The command

A>**DIR B: (cr)**

names the files on the disk in drive B, while keeping you logged on to drive A. Most versions of DOS will indicate the amount of disk space used by each file when the DIR command is invoked.

If the directory of filenames on the disk in the A drive is several screens long, the command

A>**DIR/P (cr)**

will immediately display the first screen. Then, striking any key will produce the second screen, and so forth. Alternatively, the command

A>**DIR/W (cr)**

displays filenames only, allowing you to scan over 100 filenames at a time (5 across).

DIR is an internal command.

Changing the Logged Drive

If you are currently logged on to the A drive the command

A>**B: (cr)**

switches you to the disk in drive B. You should observe that the computer will now prompt with

B> (or B:)

To switch back to drive A, just type

B>**A:** **(cr)**

This command is also internal.

Copying a File

A command such as

A>**COPY FILE1 FILE2** **(cr)**

will take a file named FILE1 on the disk in drive A and copy it to a file named FILE2 on the same disk. In a two-drive system, if we had wanted to copy FILE1 from the disk in drive A to another disk in drive B and name it FILE2 on the B-drive disk, we could have issued the command

A>**COPY FILE1 B:FILE2** **(cr)**

To copy FILE1 to the B drive disk without changing its name, use the command

A>**COPY FILE1 B:** **(cr)**

To change the name of a file without copying it, use another DOS command, RENAME, as follows

A>**REN FILE1 FILE2** **(cr)**

Both COPY and RENAME are internal commands.

Copying the Entire Contents of a Disk

The DISKCOPY command lets you copy the entire contents of one disk onto another disk. Like FORMAT, DISKCOPY is an external command.

With a two-drive system, place your DOS disk in drive A and issue the command

A>**DISKCOPY A: B:** **(cr)**

This command will enable you to copy the contents of the disk in drive A to the disk in drive B. The system will then prompt you as follows:

Insert source diskette in drive A:
Insert target diskette in drive B:
Strike any key when ready_

At this point, exchange the DOS disk in drive A with your source disk. Also, put the target disk in drive B. Then strike any key.

In many versions of DOS, the DISKCOPY command formats as it copies. Note that DISKCOPY, like FORMAT, erases any files already on the target disk.

Erasing Files

A command such as

A>**ERASE FILE1** (cr)

erases FILE1 from the disk in drive A. It is particularly useful to erase unwanted files from a disk that is reaching capacity. In a two-drive system, if the default drive is A and FILE1 is in drive B, you can issue the command

A>**ERASE B:FILE1** (cr)

Erase is an internal command.

Determining the Amount of Free Disk Space

The CHKDSK (for *CHecK DiSK*) command is used to check the remaining free space on the disk in the default drive. For example, issue

A>**CHKDSK** (cr)

if you wish to check the remaining free space on the disk in drive A. If, on the other hand, you wish to check the remaining space on the disk in the B drive, issue the command in the form

A>**CHKDSK B:** (cr)

After the CHKDSK command is executed, you'll be provided with useful information such as that below:

```
362496   bytes total disk space
 78848   bytes in 1 user files
283648   bytes available on disk

260096   bytes total memory
235520   bytes free
```

Thus, the disk in this example has over 283 KB available.

CHKDSK is an external DOS command.

Invoking an Applications Software Package

The command you must issue depends on the particular package you wish to summon once you are in DOS. Below are the commands applicable to the software covered in this *Guide:*

A>**WS** (cr) {Invokes WordStar

A>**123** (cr)
A>**LOTUS** (cr) {Both invoke 1-2-3

A>**DBASE** (cr) {Invokes either dBASE II or dBASE III

To invoke a package, remove your DOS disk from the A drive when you have an A> prompt. Next, load the applications software disk into the A drive and the disk to contain your own files into the B drive. Then issue the appropriate command, as shown above.

There is a hierarchical relationship between DOS and the applications software packages (see Figure 2-3). DOS is a gateway program that, in addition to managing disk operations, is both the entry point into and exit point out of any applications software package. If, for example, you're currently using WordStar and want to use 1-2-3, you must first exit WordStar to DOS and then go from DOS to 1-2-3. Later, you'll learn how to exit each of these packages to return to DOS.

You should also note that each of the packages shown in Figure 2-3—DOS, WordStar, 1-2-3, and dBASE—completely takes over your computer system when it is active. For example, WordStar has a set of commands that work only in WordStar. Also, when WordStar is active, it completely takes over your keyboard, making it respond in a certain way. Later, if you use 1-2-3, WordStar commands won't work. And, of course, 1-2-3 causes your keyboard to act differently than it did under WordStar control.

NAMING FILES

In addition to the DOS commands we've described, you must be familiar with the rules for naming DOS files. Because it is DOS that must manage the files on your disk, any applications software that interfaces with DOS must follow DOS's file-naming conventions.

Consider, for example

B:NAME1.MON

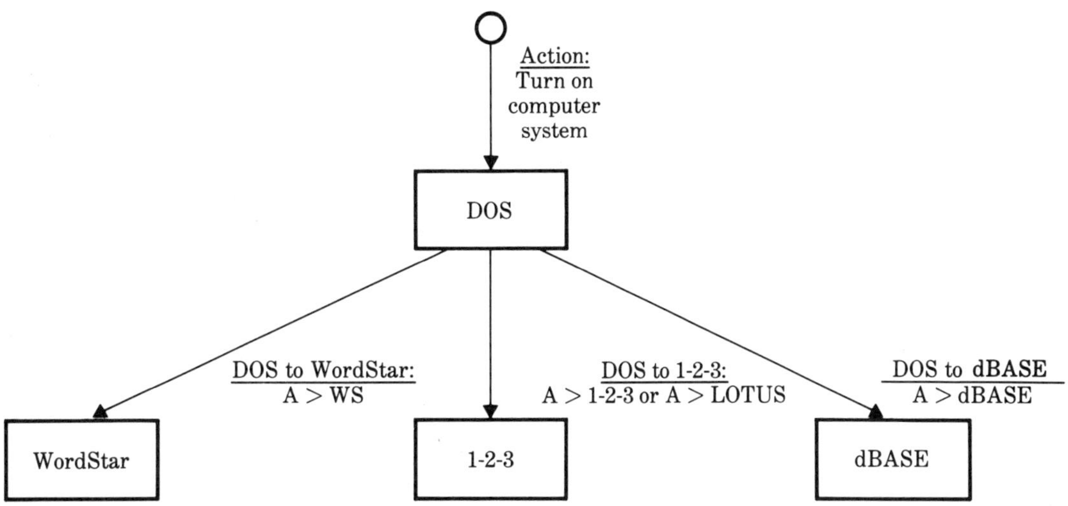

Figure 2-3. The hierarchical relationship between DOS, WordStar, and dBASE.

A *filename,* such as this one, consists of three possible components, separated respectively by a colon and a period. The first (optional and temporary) component is the drive on which the file resides. Some software packages automatically assume that you'll be saving and retrieving files on the A drive, unless you specify otherwise. To alert the package to point instead to the B drive when saving or retrieving files you must either invoke such an option when you get into the package or explicitly type in the letter B as part of the filename (as shown in the example above).

The next (mandatory) component is the main part of the filename, which consists of 1 to 8 characters. In many software packages, this part of the filename must begin with a letter and cannot contain special characters. If you type a name that exceeds eight characters, DOS will truncate (eliminate) all characters after the first eight.

The third (optional) component is the *extension* to the main part of the filename, which consists of 1 to 3 characters. The extension is useful to qualify related files; for example,

DATAF1.MON
DATAF1.TUE
DATAF1.WED

Special Extensions

Many productivity software packages automatically add their own extensions to certain files as they save them. For example, WordStar uses the extension .BAK (for *backup*) on filenames that are saved more than once. So, for example, if you type a letter and save it under the name JOHN, and then make some corrections to the letter and save it again, the latest version of the letter will have the filename JOHN and the earlier version the filename JOHN.BAK.

1-2-3 uses the extension .WKS (for *worksheet*) on every worksheet that you create with it. For each *graph* you create, it uses the extension .PIC. Because 1-2-3 can tell by context whether you are working on a worksheet or a graph, you will not be explicitly creating or referring to extensions when working with 1-2-3.

Like 1-2-3, dBASE also appends special extensions to all of your files. Two dBASE extensions that you'll need to become familiar with as you read this *Guide* are .DBF and .NDX. The extension DBF is used for most of the files you'll create, whereas NDX is used for *index files,* which help you arrange data.

When you are logged onto either 1-2-3 or dBASE you should *not* explicitly refer to the extensions when handling their associated files. For example, if you are using 1-2-3 and want to save a worksheet named INCOME, save it as

INCOME

If you later retrieve or erase it while logged onto 1-2-3, again refer to it as INCOME. Although it is saved on disk as INCOME.WKS, 1-2- 3 assumes that every worksheet you are processing has a .WKS extension. However, if you want to do something with INCOME when you are in DOS, then you must refer to this file as INCOME.WKS. DOS does not assume any particular file extension, since it works with so many software packages. Thus, you must always declare the filename with its extension (if any exists) when in DOS.

Global Identifiers

You should learn at the outset to be systematic when naming files. For example, let's say you're creating with WordStar a 10-chapter book (using 10 files). You later want to make copies of the most current versions of each chapter (i.e., those without .BAK extensions) on another disk. If you had named each chapter with the same extension (say, for example, CUR), as shown below

CH01.CUR
CH02.CUR
CH03.CUR
etc.

you could use a single COPY command to copy all 10 of these files—and only these 10 files—to another disk. To do this, put the source disk in the A drive and the target disk in the B drive. Then issue the command

A>**COPY CH*.CUR B: (cr)**

(Remember, COPY is an internal command, so your DOS disk does not have to be present in the A drive.)

The * character, when used in DOS filenames, is a *global identifier.* Since the main part of the filename can consist of up to 8 characters, we are telling DOS to copy *all* files having CH as the first two letters in the main part of the filename and CUR as an extension to the B drive.

The global identifier also works with the ERASE command.

Section 3

WordStar

WordStar is probably the most well-known and widely used word processing package in existence today. It was first released in 1981, which places it squarely among the earliest, still-surviving word processors available for use on microcomputers. It was originally designed to run on 8-bit computers using the CP/M operating system. Today, versions of WordStar exist for most 16-bit microcomputers.

Compared to many other word processors, especially some of the more recent ones, WordStar is widely thought of as being more difficult to learn. Many of its commands involve depressing three keys, and some of the key sequences are not so easy to remember if you are not using the package on a regular basis. Additionally, when WordStar text is displayed on screen, it may include a confusing array of specialized command symbols. Nonetheless, the English language is considered difficult to master, too, so if you can read a typical newspaper or magazine, you really should have no difficulty learning and using WordStar.

WHAT WORDSTAR DOES

WordStar, like many word processors available today, will enable you to prepare rapidly most types of text material—for example, letters, lists, term papers, formatted reports, and even books (such as this textbook, which was completely developed on WordStar). You are able to work rapidly because everything you type is recorded electronically. This lets you add, erase, insert, copy, move, reformat, and search for materials with a minimum of keystrokes.

Besides being able to easily "cut and paste" a document together, WordStar is designed to be used in concert with a wide variety of microcomputer-oriented printers to produce draft-quality, quickly printed documents or letter-quality, slowly prepared ones. Depending on your printer, other print styles may also be available. And of course, since documents are saved on disk, you can output them again and again, in different print styles if you wish.

Despite the fact that WordStar is a highly viable tool for secretaries, authors, and virtually anyone else who has need for a typewriter, it does have a number of limitations. First, it is cumbersome to use for tasks such as preparing mailing labels and form letters. To do tasks such as these through WordStar you would need to acquire an *add-on package*. For example,

MicroPro International Corporation (WordStar's vendor) offers a companion program called MailMerge, which is specifically targeted to users with these needs. Other firms offer similar types of add-on packages that can be used with WordStar.

Other limitations to WordStar are that it doesn't sort (a feature that can be handy if you need to manipulate alphabetized lists), footnote, or permit you to work in a variety of specialized graphical fonts. Again, you would need to acquire the appropriate add-on packages to do these. Micropro International does have a spelling checker (called SpellStar) that is available with WordStar but, like MailMerge, this program is separately priced.

Despite the fact that WordStar is not an all-purpose type of word processor, it does have several compelling advantages. For example, when you hit a snag, there's the consolation of knowing that a quick solution is probably within walking distance. There are more WordStar users around than users of any other word processing package. Also, WordStar is relatively free of bugs. This can be very important, as anyone knows who has ever had a package fail, taking several hour's worth of work with it. Finally there's the issue of interfaces with other software. Because WordStar is so widely used, many routines are available to enable WordStar users to convert their files into forms that are compatible with other software products.

HOW WORDSTAR WORKS

WordStar's "trees" are its rich variety of commands, many of which can be invoked with 1 to 3 keystrokes. Its "forest" is its command menus. Here we'll take a quick look at the forest; in the next subsection, we'll closely examine the trees.

Most of the time when you are using WordStar, you'll type as you normally do on a typewriter. If you make a simple mistake, you can use the Insert and Delete keys to make corrections. However, if you want to do something out of the normal flow—such as center text, adjust margins, or search for specific words—you'll need to summon a WordStar command menu.

WordStar employs a system of *seven* command menus. The menus and a brief description of some of their functions are shown in Figure 3-1. It's not necessary for you to become familiar with the specific functions of these menus yet, but you should understand now that most of the instructions you'll issue to WordStar are done from these command menus. Only when a menu is "active" (and only a single menu can be active at a time) can you invoke the commands on it. For example, if you want to change the margins on your document, you must be at the onscreen menu. Later you'll learn how to move from one menu to another when you want to issue specific commands.

WORDSTAR MENUS

Menu	Function
Opening	Enables you to enter or edit a new or established file, control documents after editing, and quit WordStar for DOS.
Main	Enables basic document preparation and is the gateway menu to the help, quick, onscreen, block, and print menus.
Help	Enables you to adjust help level, to get onscreen explanations or more space on your screen.
Print	Enables you to create special printing effects such as boldface, underlining, subscripts, superscripts, and overprinting.
Quick	Enables you to move around a document quickly, as well as to access search and replace functions.
Block	Enables you to save or abandon files, return to the opening menu, and mark blocks of text for moving or copying.
Onscreen	Enables you to set margins, center text, and set line spacing.

Figure 3-1. The seven WordStar menus and some of their functions.

Figures 3-2 through 3-9 show what the seven menus look like when they are displayed on your monitor screen. Once you learn how to navigate around these menus you'll have mastered WordStar. The two menus that you'll be working with most are the *opening menu* (Figure 3-2) and the *main menu* (Figure 3-3).

Another thing that you should know before you load your WordStar disk is that you can't get directly to some menus from certain others. For example, there is no way to get directly from the block menu to the onscreen

```
            not editing
                < < <  O P E N I N G   M E N U  > > >
 ---Preliminary Commands---      --File Commands--     -System Commands-
L  Change logged disk drive                              R  Run a program
F  File directory   now  OFF      P  PRINT  a file       X  EXIT to system
H  Set help level
 ---Commands to open a file---    E  RENAME a file      -WordStar Options-
   D  Open a document file        O  COPY   a file       M  Run MailMerge
   N  Open a nondocument file     Y  DELETE a file       S  Run SpellStar
```

Figure 3-2. The opening menu screen.

Status line

```
   B:LETTER.DAD   PAGE 1  LINE 1  COL 01               INSERT ON
                      < < <     M A I N   M E N U      > > >
  --Cursor Movement--        | -Delete- |   -Miscellaneous-    | -Other Menus-
^S char left ^D char right   |^G  char  |^I Tab    ^B Reform   | (from Main only)
^A word left ^F word right   |DEL chr lf|^V INSERT ON/OFF      |^J Help  ^K Block
^E line up   ^X line down    |^T word rt|^L Find/Replce again  |^Q Quick ^P Print
     --Scrolling--           |^Y  line  |RETURN End paragraph  |^O Onscreen
^Z line down ^W line up      |          |^N Insert a RETURN    |
^C screen up ^R screen down  |          |^U Stop a command     |
 L----!----!----!----!----!----!----!----!----!----!----!--------R
```

Ruler line (present on all menu screens except the one for the Opening Menu)

Figure 3-3. The main menu screen.

menu. To get to either of these menus, you must be at the main menu. The navigational paths you are allowed to take when changing from one WordStar menu to another are shown in Figure 3-9.

Thus to start WordStar, you begin at the opening menu, where you name the file on which you want to work. WordStar then automatically puts you at the main menu. This is where you start typing the document. In the course of typing text, if you need to do anything special (such as changing from single to double space, indenting a specific block of text, centering text, or resetting tab stops), you call up one of the five low-level menus shown in Figure 3-9 and issue a specialized command from that menu. Then, generally, you are automatically returned to the main menu screen, where you can resume typing text. Once you get this routine down, using WordStar is really very simple.

The five low-level menus that you can call from the main menu are always invoked by depressing the Control key—denoted by the caret character (^), the most important keystroke in WordStar—followed by a letter key. For example, ^O summons the onscreen menu. If, when at the onscreen menu, you type C (see Figure 3-5), the text appearing on the cursor

```
^Q     B:LETTER.DAD   PAGE 1  LINE 1  COL 01               INSERT ON
                        < < <    Q U I C K   M E N U      > > >
  ---Cursor Movement---        | -Delete- | --Miscellaneous--  | --Other Menus--
 S left side  D right side     |Y line  rt| F Find text in file| (from Main only)
 E top scrn   X bottom scrn    |DEL lin lf| A Find & Replace   |^J Help  ^K Block
 R top file   C end file                  | L Find Misspelling |^Q Quick ^P Print
 B top block  K end block                 | Q Repeat command or|^O Onscreen
 0-9 marker   Z down  W up                |   key until space  | Space Bar returns
 P previous   V last Find or Block        |   bar or other key | you to Main Menu.
 L----!----!----!----!----!----!----!----!----!----!----!--------R
```

Figure 3-4. The quick menu screen.

```
^O       B:LETTER.DAD   PAGE 1  LINE 1  COL 01              INSERT ON
                        < < <     O N S C R E E N  M E N U    > > >
-Margins & Tabs-     | -Line Functions-    |  --More Toggles--   |  -Other Menus-
L Set left margin    | C Center text       | J Justify   now ON  | (from Main only)
R Set right margin   | S Set line spacing  | V Vari-Tabs now ON  |^J Help  ^K Block
X Release margins    |                     | H Hyph-help now ON  |^Q Quick ^P Print
I Set  N Clear tab   |    ---Toggles---    | E Soft hyph now OFF |^O Onscreen
G Paragraph tab      | W Wrd wrap now ON   | D Prnt disp now ON  | Space Bar returns
F Ruler from line    | T Rlr line now ON   | P Pge break now ON  | you to Main Menu.

L----!----!----!----!----!----!----!----!----!----!----!--------R
```

Figure 3-5. The onscreen menu screen.

```
^J       B:LETTER.DAD   PAGE 1  LINE 1  COL 01              INSERT ON
                          < < <    H E L P  M E N U     > > >
                                            |                    |--Other Menus--
 H  Display & set the help level            | S  Status line     |(from Main only)
 B  Paragraph reform (CONTROL-B)            | R  Ruler line      |^J Help   ^K Block
 F  Flags in rightmost column               | M  Margins & Tabs  |^Q Quick  ^P Print
 D  Dot commands, print controls            | P  Place markers   |^O Onscreen
 I  Index of commands                       | V  Moving text     | Space Bar returns
                                            |                    | you to Main Menu

L----!----!----!----!----!----!----!----!----!----!----!--------R
```

Figure 3-6. The help menu screen.

```
^K       B:LETTER.DAD   PAGE 1  LINE 1  COL 01              INSERT ON
                          < < <    B L O C K  M E N U    > > >
-Saving Files-     | -Block Operations-  | -File Operations-     |  --Other Menus--
S  Save & resume   | B  Begin  K  End    | R  Read   P  Print    |  (from Main only)
D  Save--done      | H  Hide / Display   | O  Copy   E  Rename   |  ^J Help   ^K Block
X  Save & exit     | C  Copy   Y  Delete | J  Delete             |  ^Q Quick  ^P Print
Q  Abandon file    | V  Move   W  Write  | -Disk Operations-     |  ^O Onscreen
-Place Markers-    | N  Column  now OFF  | L  Change logged disk |  Space Bar returns
0-9 set/hide 0-9   |                     | F  Directory now OFF  |  you to Main Menu

L----!----!----!----!----!----!----!----!----!----!----!--------R
```

Figure 3-7. The block menu screen.

```
^P       B:LETTER.DAD   PAGE 1  LINE 1  COL 01              INSERT ON
                          < < <    P R I N T  M E N U    > > >
 ------ Special   Effects ------     -Printing Changes-          --Other Menus--
(begin and end)  |  (one time each)   | A  Alternate pitch       | (from Main only)
B Bold D Double  | H  Overprint char  | N  Standard pitch        | ^J Help   ^K Block
 S  Underscore   | O  Non-break space | C  Printing pause        | ^Q Quick  ^P Print
 X  Strikeout    | F  Phantom space   | Y  Other ribbon color    | ^O Onscreen
 V  Subscript    | G  Phantom rubout  |  --User Patches--        |  Space Bar returns
 T  Superscript  | RET  Overprint line| Q(1)  W(2)  E(3)  R(4)   |  you to Main Menu

L----!----!----!----!----!----!----!----!----!----!----!--------R
```

Figure 3-8. The print menu screen.

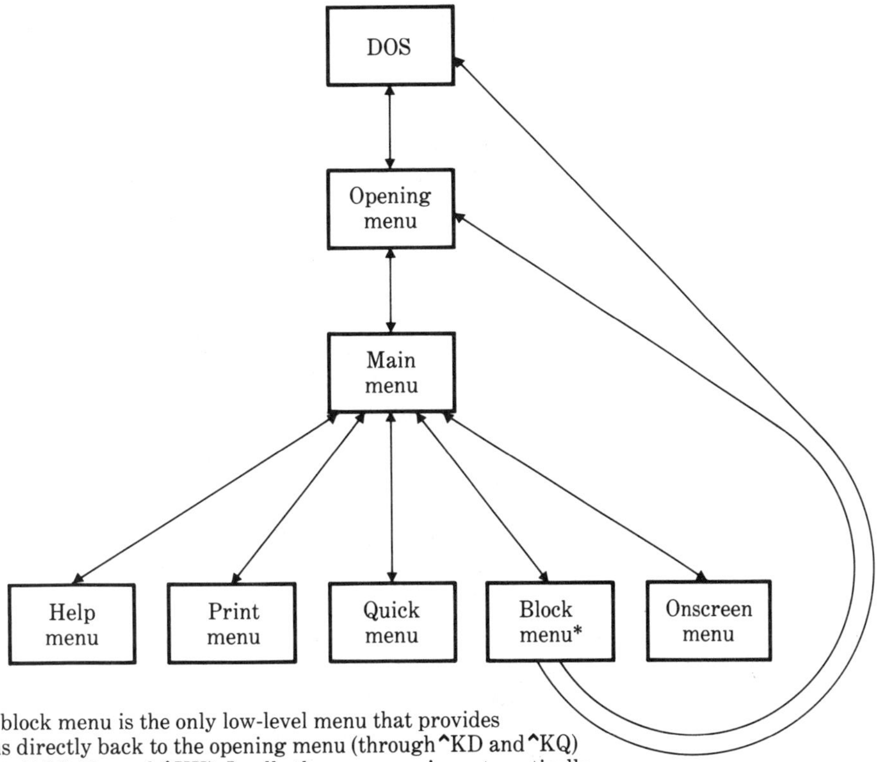

*The block menu is the only low-level menu that provides paths directly back to the opening menu (through ^KD and ^KQ) and to DOS (through ^KX). In all other cases you're automatically returned to the main menu from a low-level menu.

Figure 3-9. Navigational paths for WordStar menus.

line will be centered. And as already stated, WordStar then automatically returns you to the main menu so normal typing can resume.

The Control key works like a typewriter's shift key. So for example, to key in a WordStar command such as ^**OC**, you depress the **Control** key and (leaving your finger on it) hit the **O** key and (next) the **C** key.

GETTING STARTED: YOUR FIRST WORDSTAR EXERCISES

Now that you have an overview of how WordStar is organized, let's get familiar with some specific commands. In this subsection you'll be typing a short letter and performing some simple editing operations on it. Later on we'll look at some other operations you might want to execute with WordStar.

Invoking WordStar

The version of WordStar you'll be using is probably installed on a single floppy disk. When you get DOS's A> prompt, place the WordStar program disk in the A drive and the disk you want to contain your WordStar documents in the B drive. Then, type in the command

A>**WS** **(cr)**

What appears next on your monitor is a temporary screen announcing the version of WordStar you are using, followed by a screen with WordStar's opening menu (refer to Figure 3-2).

Changing the Logged Drive

Most people who use WordStar want the documents they prepare sent to the B drive. Thus WordStar must be informed at once that it is to use the B drive whenever a document is to be saved or retrieved. You can do this from the opening menu by typing

LB: **(cr)**

If you do not issue this command, WordStar will use the A drive as the default drive, and any file you want saved to or retrieved from the B drive must be referred to using B: at the beginning of the filename.

Typing a Letter

Now that you are logged onto WordStar and have it pointed to the B drive for your files, follow the procedures below:

STEP 1. Depress the **d** key (upper- or lowercase). This indicates that you want to either create a new document or retrieve an old one. The **d** is for *d*ocument file. Most WordStar users work only with document files, as these are the types of files used to prepare letters, papers, and books.

STEP 2. When the screen changes, you should see the prompt

NAME OF FILE TO EDIT?

Type

LETTER.DAD **(cr)**

Again, it doesn't matter if the letters are upper- or lowercase. If you make an error while typing the filename, use the **Backspace** key to erase unwanted characters from the screen. (The Backspace key won't erase characters when you are typing a WordStar document, but it does erase characters when you are naming files.)

What you've just typed—LETTER.DAD—is the filename that will be used to store your letter. This filename can be any acceptable DOS filename.

STEP 3. When the screen changes, you'll see the main menu at the top of your screen (refer to Figure 3-3) and, possibly, the message INSERT ON in the upper-right-hand corner. You'll also find the full name of your file

(B:LETTER.DAD) on the top line, as well as the current position of the screen cursor. The top line is sometimes called the *status line* because it displays several characteristics relating to the current document and the cursor position.

You'll also note a string of hyphens (-) and exclamation marks (!). This line is called the *ruler line.* The L that starts the line represents the left-hand margin; the R that ends the line represents the right-hand margin; and the ! marks represent the tab stops. You can get to any of the tab stops by depressing the **Tab** key (refer to Figure 2-2). Later, you'll learn how to change this ruler line if it's unsuitable to your needs.

STEP 4. Now it's time to prepare the letter. As you type in the letter, depress the **Enter** key only when you want to begin a new paragraph or skip a line. You do not need to (and generally *should not*) depress the Enter key at all within each paragraph itself. WordStar, like most word processors, automatically puts the screen cursor on the next line when the rightmost margin is encountered. This is called a *soft carriage return,* in contrast to the *hard carriage return* you produce when you place the screen cursor on the next line by hitting the Enter key. Incidentally, if you make a mistake, just continue typing. We'll deal with correcting mistakes later.

So if you're ready to begin, type the letter shown in Figure 3-10. You can use your keyboard's Tab key to indent the first sentence of each paragraph.

Correcting Mistakes

As you were typing the letter there are a number of things that could have gone wrong. For example, you may have misspelled a word or accidentally erased a line. Corrections are often made by using the *arrow keys* (refer to Figure 2-2) to position the cursor at the point of the error and then issuing an editing command. Two of the most common ways to correct errors are by using the Delete key and the Insert key.

```
Dear Dad,

     I'm taking an exciting computer class and we're learning how
to create documents with WordStar.  If I work hard in the class,
I should learn how to write my term papers, and even a computer
book, on a word processor.

     That's all for now.  It's time to get back to my studies.

Sincerely,


Your Favorite Child
```

Figure 3-10. A simple letter.

DELETE KEY. Suppose you spelled "term" as "terrm". To correct the mistake, use the **arrow keys** to move the cursor to the "m" character in "terrm". Then, depress the **Delete** key. Note that the character to the left of the "m"—the second "r"—is deleted. Also, all characters to the right of the cursor are shifted over one space to the left. In WordStar, the Delete key always removes the character to the *left* of the cursor.

Some people prefer deleting characters *at* the cursor position instead. This can be done by moving to the character you wish to delete, and holding down the **Control** key while hitting the **G** key (that is, **^G**).

INSERT KEY. In WordStar, the **Insert** key is a toggle key (see page 9 for a discussion of toggle keys). Try pressing it on and off for a few seconds and notice the appearance and subsequent disappearance of the INSERT ON message. When INSERT ON is activated, you can insert characters; when it's off, you can't.

To see how inserting works, suppose you misspelled "term" as "tem". To insert the missing "r" in the proper place, again use the **arrow keys** to set the cursor to the "m". Then, with the INSERT ON feature visible on the status line, hit the **r** key. Note that the "r" is inserted at the cursor position and all text immediately to the right is pushed one space to the right.

Often text will have a ragged-looking appearance if you do a lot of insertion and deletion. You can later correct this by letting WordStar reformat your document. Reformatting will be discussed on page 31.

Before we move on, you should note that another common mistake is summoning the wrong menu. When this happens, depress the **Escape** key to bail out of the situation.

Saving Documents

After you've finished typing LETTER.DAD and correcting it, you'll next need to save it on disk. Saving is done from the block menu.

To save a document and return to the opening menu type

^KD

The ^K tells WordStar that you want to issue a command on the block menu. As you'll note in Figure 3-7, the D indicates that you are done with the document and want to save it.

If you aren't done with your document and want to return to it after saving it, you should type

^KS

Most experienced users will issue this command every several pages in a document, so that if something unforeseen happens—such as an electrical spike hitting a power line (which is not unusual in a lightning storm) or a brownout, both of which could zap your main memory—at least all of the document up to the latest save operation will be on disk.

Keep in mind that the save command always takes the main memory contents of the file you are working on and writes them *over* the contents of the file on disk stored under the same name. In principle, saving works exactly like recording one music album over another on a cassette tape.

Retrieving Documents

The two most common retrieval situations you'll encounter are:

- retrieving a document when you first invoke WordStar
- "quitting" one document so you can retrieve another

Looking at the first situation, let's say it's tomorrow and you want to retrieve LETTER.DAD and work on it further. To do this, load DOS and invoke WordStar in the usual way. Again, tell WordStar to use the B drive for all of your files.

Next, type **d** from the opening menu. When WordStar prompts

NAME OF FILE TO EDIT?

type **LETTER.DAD** and hit the **Enter** key. WordStar will then look for the file on disk and, if it's found, it will appear on the display screen. If it's not found, WordStar will give you another chance to enter a filename. Incidentally, if you suddenly realize that you forgot to save LETTER.DAD, and you want to bail out of the prompt, hit the **Escape** key to return to the opening menu.

Looking at the second retrieval situation listed above, suppose you were working on another document and wanted to retrieve LETTER.DAD, without saving your current document. You would use the command **^KQ** to "quit" what you're doing and return to the opening menu. Here, you can retrieve LETTER.DAD in the manner already described. If you had wanted instead to save your current document, you could have used the **^KD** command described earlier.

Printing Documents

To print a WordStar document, the document must first be saved on disk. If you are at the opening menu, you can print a document by typing

P

At the prompt that next appears, supply the name of the document—LETTER.DAD—and hit the **Enter** key. You'll then be asked a series of simple questions, which you can answer, or you can simply press the **Escape** key if you wish to print the document in its entirety. If you wish to answer some questions but not others, depress the **Enter** key when the cursor is at a question you wish to skip.

You can also print a document from the main menu by typing

^KP

The first two keystrokes (^K) invoke the block menu. The third (P) issues the print command from this menu.

Leaving WordStar

If you've done all you wanted with WordStar and want to get back to DOS, you can do it in several ways. If you are at the opening menu, simply type **X**. If you are at the main menu and want to save your current document before returning to the operating system, type **^KX.** If, on the other hand, you don't want to save the document, type **^KQ** (to get back to the opening menu) followed by **X**.

OTHER USEFUL WORDSTAR OPERATIONS

There are so many other useful WordStar commands that it would take a full book to adequately cover them all. But, as mentioned earlier, you don't have to know every command (or even most of them) to do respectable work with this package. Here are a number of widely used WordStar commands to supplement some of the elementary ones you've already picked up.

Moving the Cursor

There are many ways to move the cursor around a WordStar document. Using the arrow keys, already mentioned, is one of them. Other useful ways are shown in the table below:

When you...	The cursor moves...
type **^F**	right one word
type **^A**	left one word
press the **Home** key	to top of screen
press the **End** key	to bottom of screen
type **^QR**	to top of document
type **^QC**	to bottom of document
press the **PgUp** key	to same relative position on previous screen page
press the **PgDn** key	to same relative position on next screen page

Deleting Lines

Typing **^Y** will delete the line on which the cursor is positioned. All lines that were originally below that line will then move up one line. Holding down the Control key while repeatedly invoking ^Y will delete several lines below the cursor line. A paragraph can be deleted quickly this way.

Inserting Lines

A document's appearance can be enhanced significantly by inserting blank lines at places where text is crowded. To insert a line, first make sure INSERT ON is invoked (using the **Insert** key if necessary). Then use the

arrow keys to place the cursor after the last character in the line you want followed by a blank line (or, alternatively, at the position of the first character in the line you want preceded by a blank line) and hit the **Enter** key. Hitting the Enter key several more times will produce several blank lines.

Reformatting Text

This is one of the most important operations in WordStar. As you repeatedly insert and delete text, the righthand margin will no longer look presentable. Insertion often pushes text beyond the righthand margin, while deletion pulls text away from this margin. To correct this odd-looking appearance, you'll need to *reformat* the document. Reformatting makes the document look like you had typed it in directly, with each line filled.

To reformat, go to the first character in the paragraph that looks sloppy and type **^B**. If the hyphen-help toggle (**^OH**) is on, WordStar will stop at the end of some lines to ask if you want to hyphenate and break a long word that extends beyond the right margin. If you do, depress the **Hyphen** key and WordStar will hyphenate the word and continue reformatting until it comes to the end of the paragraph or another candidate for hyphenation. If you don't want to hyphenate a word, hit **^B** again and the entire word will move to the next line. If the hyphen-help toggle is off, WordStar will automatically square up (i.e., reformat within the margins) all text between the cursor and the next hard carriage return. Most WordStar users prefer working with the hyphen-help toggle *off*.

Usually, the hard carriage return is at the end of the paragraph, placed there when you hit the return key to start a new paragraph. If the next paragraph needs reformatting, make sure the cursor is at its beginning and type ^B again. Keep on doing this until the entire document looks attractive.

You can also reformat a document from single- to double-spacing (or vice versa). This operation is discussed on page 32.

Justification

WordStar users can have text formatted with a "flush" or "ragged" right edge. If you choose the flush right edge, WordStar will insert some extra blank spaces between words on each line so that the last character in every line is flush against the right margin. Some people like documents with this look, but many people find the extra blanks between words distracting. For business correspondence, most people prefer a ragged right edge.

Some installed versions of WordStar default to the flush right edge. If you want a ragged edge, type

^OJ

This is a toggle command, so typing ^OJ a second time reverts back to the flush edge. If the right edge on your document is flush and you want it ragged (or vice versa), you must use the reformat command (^B) to correct it appropriately.

As an exercise, you should try reformatting LETTER.DAD from the flush right edge to a ragged right edge (or vice versa).

Centering Text

Type the text you want centered on one line. Leaving the cursor on the same line, invoke **^OC**. The text on this line will then automatically be centered.

Indenting a Paragraph

Suppose you want to indent the text of an entire paragraph a total of 5 spaces (i.e., one tab stop inward) from the leftmost margin. Before you begin the paragraph, invoke **^OG**. Every line of text subsequently typed will be indented 5 spaces, until a hard carriage return is made. At that point ^OG is negated. If you want, instead, to indent 10 spaces from the left (that is, two tab stops), just invoke ^OG twice. Again, a hard carriage return forces the cursor back to the original left-margin position.

On the IBM PC, the F2 function key will automatically invoke the ^OG keystrokes.

Hanging Indents

Say you have a list of remarks numbered 1., 2., and so forth (as the "Notes" at the bottom of the expense summary in Exercise 6 or the remarks in Figure 12-9c on page 361 of *Understanding Computers and Data Processing*). Type the **1.** flush against the left margin and then invoke **^OG** (or depress the **F2** function key on the IBM PC). All of the text that follows will be indented until a hard carriage return is made. Then type **2.** and repeat the process. Do the same for all the items on the list.

Double-Spacing

To double-space, invoke **^OS**. WordStar will then ask for a number to be typed in, representing the spacing desired. A **2** will give double-spacing, a **3** triple-spacing, and so on. After the appropriate digit has been typed, WordStar will comply with the requested line spacing until commanded to do otherwise.

If a single-spaced document later needs to be double-spaced, all is not lost. Request double-spacing as already described. Then go through the document paragraph by paragraph, invoking the ^B command to automatically reformat the document. To see if you really understand how this works, try changing the line spacing of the letter in Figure 3-10, from single- to double-spaced.

Moving and Copying

Most people who word process documents have a need to move a block of text from one location to another, or to replicate a block of text one or more times. To accomplish either of these operations, the block of text to be moved or copied must first be *marked.* To mark a block of text, you need to put a marker at both the beginning and end of the block.

For example, let's return to the letter you prepared in the previous subsection. Suppose we want to change the order of the sentences in the last paragraph. In other words, we want the last paragraph to read

> It's time to get back to my studies. That's
> all for now.

To do this, we must *move* the second sentence in front of the first one. This can be accomplished by positioning the cursor at the "I" character of the word "It's" and typing

^KB

As you'll notice, this places a marker (<B>) at the beginning of the sentence. Next, we position the cursor behind the period in the second sentence and invoke

^KK

At this point, depending on your monitor, either a second marker (<K>) will appear at the end of the sentence, or the marked sentence will be displayed in a manner different from the rest of the letter, or the first marker will disappear. In any case, the text will be marked.

To move the text you've just marked, position the cursor at the beginning of the first sentence (under the "T" in "That's") and type

^KV

This is the actual move command. Note that the order of the sentences has now been switched. Also, the block markers (<B> and <K>) should no longer be present.

Copying involves marking a block in the same way as you would in a move operation, but instead of typing ^KV, you type

^KC

Copying will replicate the block of text into a new position, while leaving a copy of it in its original position.

Inserting Files

Often a need will arise to insert the contents of one document somewhere into the contents of another.

For example, suppose you wanted to send a copy of your current class schedule to friends and relatives, including your dad. Let's assume that you stored this schedule on the B drive in a file called "SCHEDULE" and that SCHEDULE contains a lead-in sentence (such as "Here is my current class schedule . . .) followed by the schedule itself. We'll also assume that you want the text in this file placed between the first and second paragraphs of LETTER.DAD.

To insert the file, move the cursor to column 1 on the blank line between the first and second paragraphs of LETTER.DAD. Then type

^KR

WordStar will next respond

NAME OF FILE TO READ?

Type

SCHEDULE (cr)

You will then observe WordStar searching for SCHEDULE on the B drive and, upon finding it, inserting SCHEDULE into the specified place. This is a copy operation, so the original version of SCHEDULE remains unaltered.

Searching for Text

This handy operation will enable you to rapidly search a document for one or more occurrences of a particular string of characters. For example, let's go back to the letter in Figure 3-10. Suppose you want to find out if you used the word "learn" (and any derivatives of that word, such as "learning") in the letter.

To accomplish this, summon the document from the opening menu in the usual way. As soon as you are brought to the main menu, type

^QF

When WordStar responds

FIND?

type

learn (cr)

WordStar will then respond with

OPTIONS?

In this *Guide* we'll talk about three search options you can select in WordStar, denoted respectively by u, g, and n. (You can hit the **Enter** key if you wish none of these options.) At this point type

u (cr)

This tells WordStar to ignore the distinction between upper- and lowercase letters when doing the string search. WordStar will then search for the string of characters you specified, respecting blanks. This search would produce strings such as "learn," "Learn", "LEARN", "learning", and "LEARNing".

Be careful when you type in the search string. For example, if you had typed in "learn " (with a blank space as the sixth character in the string), Wordstar would fail to flag the word "learning" (which has an "i" in the sixth character position).

After you type the options requested, WordStar will next look for the first occurrence of the 5-character string. Type

^L

if you want to search for further occurrences; otherwise, hit the **Escape** key. If no occurrences of the search string are found, WordStar will notify you of this.

Searching and Replacing

Often one searches for a string of text with the thought of replacing it with another string. For example, people often find that they have consistently misspelled a word and want to replace it with the correctly spelled word. Or, writers will use an abbreviation for a long word and replace it later with the actual word.

For example, when the text accompanying the *Guide* was prepared, the word "asynchronous" appeared several times in one of the sections of Chapter 7. To save time entering this word and checking each occurrence of it for spelling errors, the string "aaa" was typed in its place. When the chapter section was finished, WordStar's search-and-replace feature was then summoned. This was done by first entering the command

^QA

WordStar then responded

FIND?

Whereupon the typist responded

aaa (cr)

At this point, WordStar countered with

REPLACE WITH?

The typist's response was

asynchronous (cr)

WordStar then responded with

OPTIONS?

Since it was desired to replace all occurrences of "aaa" with "asynchronous", with no approval needed from the operator to inspect each occurrence before it was replaced, the final typist response was

gn (cr)

The "g" here stands for a "global replacement"; the "n" stands for "no operator approval." WordStar then made the appropriate substitutions.

Changing Margins

WordStar provides a default line length of 65 characters, each line respectively starting and ending at the L (for Left) and R (for Right) character positions shown on the ruler line. But what if you want different left and right margins then the respective default margins of 1 and 65?

If, say, we want the left margin at the 20th column position and the right margin at the 50th column position we proceed as follows. To change the left margin, type

^OL20

To then change the right margin, type

^OL50

As each of these commands is issued, you'll notice the corresponding change in the ruler line.

Margin changes only affect text typed in *after* such commands are issued. But often you've already typed in some parts of a document that you want squeezed into these new margins. To adjust already typed portions, just position the cursor at the top of any paragraphs to be reformatted into the new margin boundaries and issue the reformat command, **^B**.

To see if you fully understand how to change the ruler line, try experimenting with the letter in Figure 3-10. For example, change the left and right margins to 20 and 50 (as suggested here), and then reformat the document into these new margin boundaries. Also try typing new sentences into the letter and observe what WordStar does with them.

Boldfacing and Underlining

To see how both of these printing enhancements are accomplished in WordStar, let's go back to the letter in Figure 3-10. Suppose we would like the word "exciting" in the first sentence underlined:

I'm taking an exciting computer class . . .

To do this we must mark the beginning and ending characters in "exciting" for underlining. Thus with the INSERT ON message showing in the top-right-hand corner of the screen, move the cursor to the "e" character in "exciting" and enter

^PS

Then, move to the blank space after the "g" in the same word and again enter

^PS

You'll note that ^S will remain on the screen once you've marked the word; however, when your document is later printed, these control characters will disappear and "exciting" will be underlined.

Boldfacing text is done in a similar manner, but instead of typing ^PS, type

^PB

One warning: Each ^PS (or ^PB) works as a toggle, turning underlining (boldfacing) on or off. Thus for example, if you turn the underlining feature on at the beginning of the document and forget to turn it off, nearly your whole document will be underlined.

Dot Commands

In addition to "menu commands" that can be issued through the control key, WordStar has a number of *dot commands* (see Figure 3-11). The format of these commands is a period (i.e., the "dot"), followed by two letters and (optionally) a number, text, or a keyword. For example,

.OP
.PL 84
.HE Chapter Two
.UJ OFF

The dot commands always appear on a line by themselves, at the beginning of a line, imbedded in the document you are typing on the display screen.

DOT COMMANDS

Command	Purpose
.PL	Extends or shortens page length. The default is 66 lines per page. If you are using legal-sized paper, use the command **.PL 84**
.PA	Causes an immediate page break whenever it is encountered in a document.
.OP	Causes page numbers to be suppressed.
.PN	Causes page numbers to be restored if they have previously been suppressed.
.HE	Used to place a heading at the top of every page. For example, if you are writing a paper entitled "Summer in the City," issue the command **.HE Summer in the City** on page 1, line 1 to place this heading on every page.
.FO	Used to place a footing at the bottom of every page. For example, if you wish the date 10/18/87 to appear on the bottom of every page, issue the command **.FO 10/18/87** on page 1, line 1.
.IG	Used to imbed in your WordStar file a comment that will not be printed. For example, **.IG Print five copies**

Figure 3-11. Some useful WordStar dot commands.

They are used strictly to give WordStar instructions on how to format the printed version of the document. The commands themselves do not show up in the printed output.

Creating More Screen Space

After you've worked with WordStar for a while you'll notice that the menus hog a lot of screen space that you'd like your document to occupy. The command

^JH0

will make the menus on the screen disappear, enabling you to use that screen space for your document. Although the menus are gone from the screen, they are still in force for invoking WordStar commands. If you want to see them again, just type in

^JH3

Exercises

1. Type in the letter that appears below:

```
                                  February 5, 1987


Florence L. Smythe
XYZ Corporation
30 Industrial Avenue
Pittsburgh, PA 15230

Dear Ms. Smythe:

     I certainly enjoyed my visit to XYZ company and the chat we
had there. Of course, I'm still very interested in the opening
in your accounting department and I will notify you of my
employment decision as soon as my last interview is finished next
month.

     Enclosed is a copy of a recent vita.  I apologize for not
having a copy to give you during my visit.

                                  Yours very truly,



                                  J. T. College
```

Save the letter on disk and type out a copy on your printer.

2. Make the following changes to the second paragraph of the letter in Exercise 1.

   > Enclosed ~~is a copy~~ [are two copies] of a recent vita. I [sincerely] apologize for not having ~~a copy~~ [them] to give you during my visit.

   Again, save the letter and type out a copy on your printer. Has WordStar made a backup copy of your letter (i.e., a file with a .BAK extension)?

3. Insert the following sentence as the middle paragraph in the letter of Exercise 2:

```
     Enclosed also is a list of expenses I incurred on the trip.
I would appreciate you reimbursing me at your earliest possible
convenience.
```

4. You've changed your mind in Exercise 3 and have decided to discuss expenses last. Move the paragraph on expenses from the middle paragraph to the last paragraph.
5. Double-space the text in the main body of the letter in Exercise 4 without retyping the letter.
6. Add the page below as the second page in your document. (*Hint:* Move the cursor after the last character in your letter and repeatedly depress the Enter key. As soon as you hit the page-break marker—a string of hyphens—at the end of line 55, start typing your second page.)

```
                        EXPENSES SUMMARY
                          J. T. College
                   Visit to XYZ Company, 2/2/87


1.    Airfare ....................................... $300.00
2.    Hotel ........................................    90.00
3.    Meals ........................................    65.00

      Total ........................................ $455.00

Notes
-----

1.    The airfare consisted of a round-trip coach ticket from
      Covina, CA.  I have enclosed a copy of the receipt with
      this letter.
2.    Receipt also enclosed.
3.    I lost the meal receipts but, since meals are being billed
      to my credit card, I can get receipts if you need them.
```

7. Search the two-page letter you've created in Exercise 6 for the string "XYZ" and replace each occurrence with the string "ABC".

Section 4

1-2-3

Lotus Development Corporation's 1-2-3 was one of the first *integrated software packages,** combining powerful spreadsheeting features with presentation graphics and data management capabilities. Upon its introduction in 1983 it achieved instant success. This was due largely to its friendly user interface, its ability to combine a state-of-the-art spreadsheet facility with other useful functions, and its arrival in the marketplace just as the 16-bit IBM PC and the PC-DOS (MS-DOS) operating systems were achieving popularity. Today, 1-2-3 is widely acknowledged as the best-selling electronic spreadsheet product of all time. Many loyal users still favor 1-2-3 over the newer, more sophisticated products that have arrived on the scene to compete with it.

WHAT 1-2-3 DOES

1-2-3 combines three productivity functions—spreadsheets, presentation graphics, and data management—into a single package.

An *electronic spreadsheet* (see Chapter 12 of *Understanding Computers and Data Processing* for an extensive discussion of spreadsheets) is an applications program that displays on the monitor screen a grid, which can accept text, numbers, and formulas. Most importantly the program has a *recalculation feature* that provides automatic recalculation of formulas on the grid when an interdependent cell value changes.

The *presentation graphics* feature allows users to quickly and easily graph spreadsheet data, with bar charts, pie charts, and/or line charts (also covered in Chapter 12). Normally, a chart is first prepared on the monitor screen and, if the image is satisfactory, it is saved on disk and sent to the printer.

The *data management* feature provides users with a variety of file-handling functions. Among the most notable of these are *extracting* records having specific characteristics and *sorting* records on one or more fields. In 1-2-3 each row of data is considered a *record,* while the worksheet columns are equivalent to the record's *fields.* Files, records, and fields are discussed extensively in Chapter 2 of *Understanding Computers and Data Processing.*

*An integrated software package is a software package that combines (i.e., integrates) two or more major software functions (say, spreadsheets, data management, and possibly other functions) into a single product. The advantages and disadvantages of integrated software packages are discussed on page 405 of *Understanding Computers and Data Processing.*

Despite the fact that 1-2-3 is technically an integrated software package, many people think of it primarily as a spreadsheet with ancillary features. There are two good reasons for this. First, over the last several years, presentation graphics has started to evolve as a standard feature in many spreadsheet products. Second, the data management facility is not really either a full-fledged *file manager* or a *database management system* (see Chapter 13 of *Understanding Computers and Data Processing* for a full discussion of these terms). Every record and field that you create in 1-2-3 somehow has to be fitted into the row-column format that is dictated by the physical limitations of the spreadsheet. To anyone who needs a more flexible data management tool, 1-2-3 has some serious drawbacks.

Its limitations notwithstanding, 1-2-3 has proven by its sales record to be exceptionally good at what it does best—spreadsheets. For users requiring spreadsheet support functions that are more sophisticated than those in 1-2-3, there are a number of more powerful integrated software products available. Among the most widely used of these are Lotus' Symphony, Ashton-Tate's Framework, and Micro Data Base Systems' KnowledgeMan. But beware. "Larger," more sophisticated products will generally be more expensive and more difficult to learn than 1-2-3. Such products often also require more main memory, and may also necessitate a hard disk to operate at the level of sophistication you require. Nonetheless, if you need more power than 1-2-3 provides, choosing such a product is probably your best bet.

HOW 1-2-3 WORKS

In this *Guide* we'll cover only spreadsheet and presentation graphics functions of 1-2-3. To learn how to use other aspects of the package (for example, data management routines) consult either the 1-2-3 reference manual or a trade book devoted to using 1-2-3.

In Chapter 12 of the text we introduced spreadsheets—what they do, how they work, and the terminology you'll need when working with them. Although we'll be repeating some of that discussion here, we'll be doing it quickly. Thus you may wish to go back to Chapter 12 and read pages 364–373 before starting the next subsection.

Mastering 1-2-3 involves three basic things:

- Becoming familiar with the anatomy of a worksheet and how to navigate through it
- Learning how to construct labels and values
- Understanding 1-2-3's command set

The Anatomy of a 1-2-3 Worksheet

Spreadsheet packages are used to create *worksheets*. Although electronic spreadsheet packages have existed for only about a decade or so, people like accountants have for years been manually preparing worksheets—for example, balance sheets, profit and loss statements, income tax forms, budgets, asset amortization tables, and cash flow schedules, to name just a few. Any type of schedule that combines words with numbers is, technically speaking, a worksheet. Each one that you prepare with 1-2-3 is normally saved on disk as a separate file.

Figure 4-1 illustrates the basic format of a 1-2-3 worksheet. It is a grid constructed of rows and columns, which intersect to form cells. Into any of these cells you can put words, numbers, or formulas.

Shown on the display screen in the figure are 20 rows (identified by numbers) and 8 nine-character-width columns (identified by letters). The rows and columns of the worksheet intersect to form *cells*. Each cell is addressed by its row and column coordinates. For example, cell B5 is formed by column B and row 5. You can place either text or numbers into any cell.

1-2-3 worksheets can be very large. The screen you see represents a *window* looking out on a worksheet that, in fact, consists of 2048 rows (8192 in Release 2) and 256 columns. Repeated depression or holding down of one of the four **arrow keys** will scroll other portions of the worksheet into the window. The width of any of the columns can be changed to suit the particular needs of your worksheet, as will be described later.

In 1-2-3 the screen is divided into two areas. One of these areas, the *control panel*, consists of the first three lines of the screen. It is here that you'll be developing the words and numbers to put into the cells and, also, making selections from 1-2-3's command menu. The *mode indicator* shown in the figure is controlled entirely by 1-2-3. A mode indicator of "READY,"

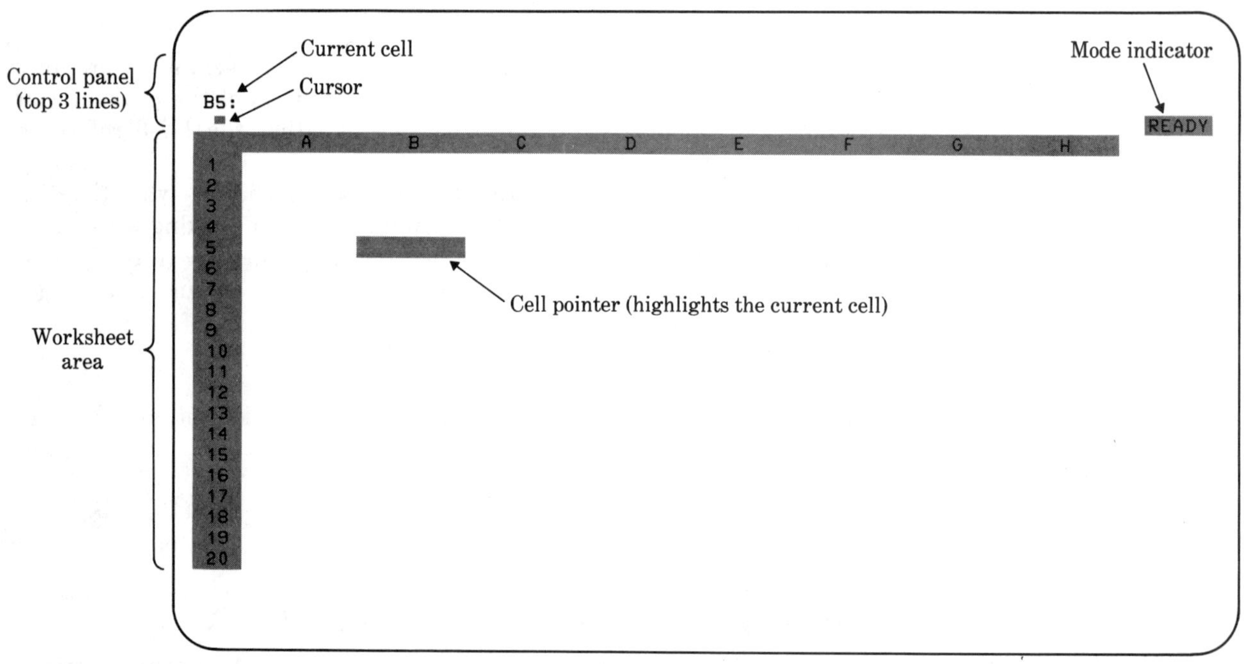

Figure 4-1. A 1-2-3 worksheet.

for example, means that 1-2-3 is ready to accept anything that you type from the keyboard, whereas a mode indicator of "WAIT" means that 1-2-3 is occupied with a calculation and will not respond to any of your keystrokes.

The other area of the screen is known as the *worksheet area.* This is the area that will eventually contain the results of your labors—the worksheet itself. As you develop entries in the control panel you send them to the worksheet area.

In many cases, you will be constructing your worksheet cell by cell. The *current cell* is the one on which you are currently working. It is the cell that the *cell pointer* is pointing to in the worksheet area. The column and row coordinates of this cell are displayed in the control panel. As you develop an entry to place into this cell, a *cursor* in the control panel will show you the position (in the control panel) where the next character you type will appear. If you make a mistake, you can use the **Backspace** key to backtrack to the point of the error and retype the rest of the entry. If you want to bail out of this cell totally, depress the **Escape** key.

Labels and Values

Every cell that you fill in on the worksheet will contain either a label or a value. *Labels* cannot be manipulated mathematically, whereas *values* can. If you think about it, every worksheet you've ever seen in your life (such as a completed income tax form or a budget) is made up of just words (labels) and numbers (values). Values can be either *numeric constants, formulas,* or *functions.* Below are some examples of labels and values:

Example	Description
Revenue	Label
Expenses	Label
.15	Numeric constant
$2,000,000	Numeric constant
.6*A5/100−B2	Formula
@SUM(A1..A4)	Function

In 1-2-3 the *first* character of a cell entry determines whether it is a label or a value. Note that:

- *Labels* always start with a letter of the alphabet (or the apostrophe character).
- *Numeric constants* and *formulas* always start with a digit, a decimal point (.), a sign character (+ or −), a pound sign (#), or a dollar sign ($). Formulas always contain "variables" (i.e., cell references) whereas numeric constants don't.
- *Functions* always start with the @ symbol.

For example, if we entered

Revenue

into a cell, it is interpreted by 1-2-3 as a label because its first character is a letter. If we wanted a label such as "1st Quarter" (which starts with a digit, and would be interpreted by 1-2-3 as a value), we would enter it as

'1st Quarter

When 1-2-3 displays this label in the worksheet area, it will get rid of the apostrophe character for you (even though that character remains in storage).

You will have the same sort of first-character recognition problem if you want to store a formula such as B2−B1, which means subtract the contents of cell B1 from the contents of cell B2 and place the result in another cell. To make sure 1-2-3 doesn't interpret this as a label, you would enter the formula as

+B2−B1

Functions are merely prestored formulas that are contained in a special library on the 1-2-3 program disk. For example, @SUM(A1..A4) means sum the values in cells A1 through A4 and place the result in another cell.

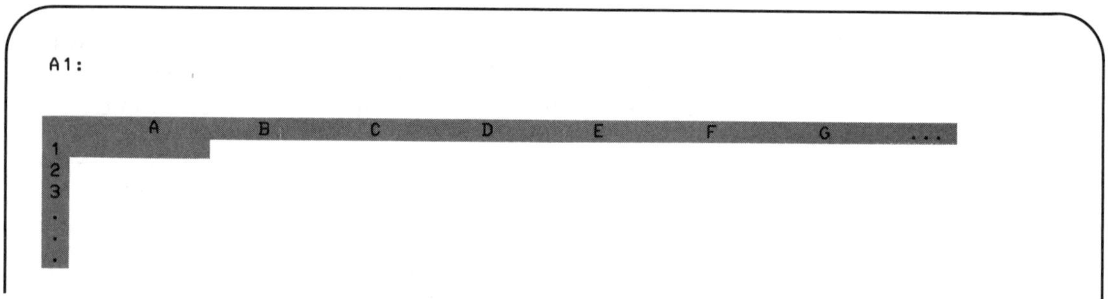

Screen 1: Before depressing the slash ("/") key

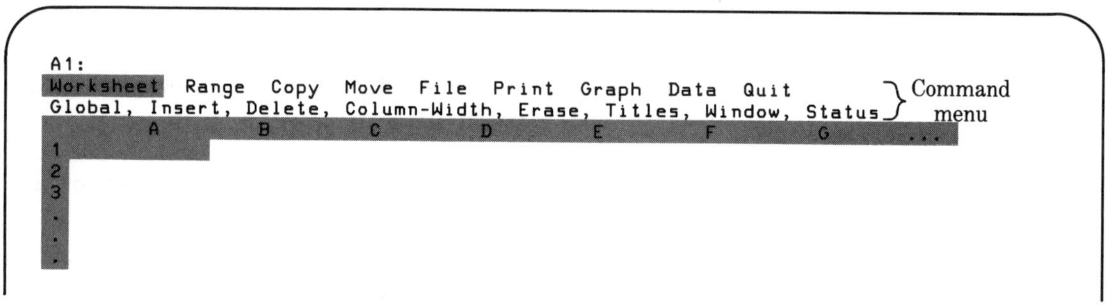

Screen 2: After depressing the slash key

Figure 4-2. Invoking the 1-2-3 command menu.

The 1-2-3 Command Set

One of the most powerful features of 1-2-3 is its *command* set. 1-2-3 has a set of *nine* commands. These commands appear in a *command menu* on the second line of the control panel when the slash (/) key is depressed (see Figure 4-2). When the command menu is summoned, the highlight on line 2 of the control panel is positioned on the command that can be *selected* by hitting the Enter key (such as "Worksheet" in the figure). Also, a description of the highlighted command appears on line 3. Figure 4-3 describes the nine 1-2-3 commands.

Later in the *Guide* we'll describe two ways to invoke 1-2-3 commands. Invoking commands in 1-2-3 involves being faced with a hierarchical set of menus. After you choose a command from the command menu you'll be provided with a series of *option menus* (or *submenus*), which ask you to choose one of several alternatives relating to the command you just selected.

1-2-3 COMMANDS

Command	Explanation
Worksheet	This command allows you to do things that affect the entire worksheet. For example, it allows you to change the width of one or more columns, and insert or delete columns or rows.
Range	This command allows you to perform operations on a portion of the worksheet.
Copy	This command allows you to reproduce any portion of the worksheet into another place on the worksheet.
Move	This command lets you relocate any portion of the worksheet into another place on the worksheet.
File	This command enables you to access your disk to save, retrieve, or combine worksheets.
Print	This command allows you to print any portion of your worksheet.
Graph	This command enables you to create graphs from your worksheet. The computer system must be equipped with a graphics display board for this command to be used effectively.
Data	This command enables you to use the data management routines, to sort data or retrieve records with specific characteristics.
Quit	This command ends your 1-2-3 session and enables you to return to DOS.

Figure 4-3. 1-2-3 commands.

For example, if we had selected the "Worksheet" command off the command menu, 1-2-3 would next provide us with a submenu of options that would enable us to do worksheet-related operations: changing the column widths on the worksheet, inserting or deleting (rows or columns) on the worksheet, and so forth. We would then select one of these submenu options and then be faced with yet another submenu. For example, if we wanted to insert, 1-2-3 would then ask us if we had a row or a column in mind.

Thus invoking commands in 1-2-3 can be seen as a process of navigating through a tree of choices. This feature makes 1-2-3 particularly easy to use. Since you can *point* to the choices on the screen, there is really no complicated command syntax to remember. The package is especially set up to enable users to apply their intuition, without constantly having to leaf through a reference manual. If you make the wrong choice in selecting an option, you can (in most cases) void the choice by hitting the Escape key, which backtracks you to the point you were at before making the choice.

GETTING STARTED: YOUR FIRST 1-2-3 EXERCISES

To familiarize you with 1-2-3, we'll produce the worksheet (a sales table) appearing in Figure 4-4. In this subsection you'll learn how to log onto 1-2-3, type in a worksheet, save it, and print it. Later we'll suggest some enhancements you can make to this worksheet to further your understanding of 1-2-3.

Invoking 1-2-3

Boot up your computer system with DOS in the usual way. When you have the A> prompt on your screen, take the DOS disk out of drive A, insert your 1-2-3 program disk, and close the drive door. Then type

A>**LOTUS (cr)**

	A	B	C	D	E ...
1	AGENT	Region A	Region B	Totals	
2	Michaels	500	200	700	
3	Adams	200	100	300	
4	Williams	50	400	450	
5	Jones	100	700	800	
6	Totals	850	1400	2250	
7					
.					
.					
.					

Figure 4-4. A sales worksheet.

What you will see next on your screen is the *Lotus Access System Menu,* with the highlight pointed to "1-2-3". 1-2-3 is the program that enables you to prepare spreadsheets. To select this option, press the **Enter** key. After a few seconds, a fresh worksheet similar to the one you saw in Figure 4-1 will appear.

Entering Labels and Numeric Constants

You are now ready to type in data for the sales table worksheet. First, type

AGENT (cr)

If you make an error as you are keying this into the control panel, use the **Backspace** key to backtrack to the point of the error and retype the remainder of the entry. After you hit the **Enter** key, you'll notice that "AGENT", a label, has been transferred to the very top line of the control panel as

'AGENT

The apostrophe is there to inform you that this entry is being stored as a label. You'll also notice that "AGENT" has been sent to cell A1 in the worksheet area.

Now use one of the **arrow keys** to move to another cell, and then type and enter the appropriate label or value. Incidentally, a faster method for entering data than the one just described is to skip the step where you depress the Enter key. Instead, when you've finished typing the contents of a cell, depress an arrow key to move on to the next cell. 1-2-3 will automatically enter any data you've typed into the control panel as soon as you depress an arrow key.

Continue in this fashion until all of the labels and values in the shaded portion of the table have been entered.

Entering Formulas

When you have finished entering all of the shaded data (that is, the labels and numeric constants), use the arrow keys to move to cell D2. This cell contains the total sales attributable to an agent named Michaels. Here we'll establish a formula to enable 1-2-3 to automatically calculate (and later recalculate) Michaels' sales for us. Since Michaels' sales total can be found by totalling the values in cells B2 and C2, type the formula

+B2+C2

Remember, we need the + sign on the front end of the formula to tell 1-2-3 that this entry is a value. After you have typed the formula, use the **down-arrow key** to enter it and move on to cell D3. Note that, upon doing this, 1-2-3 has placed the correct sum, 700, in cell D2. Now type the formula

+B3+C3

for cell D3 and enter it. In a similar fashion, move around to the other margin cells that haven't yet been totalled and enter the appropriate formulas. Note that these formulas are

cell D4: +**B4**+**C4**

cell D5: +**B5**+**C5**

cell B6: +**B2**+**B3**+**B4**+**B5**

cell C6: +**C2**+**C3**+**C4**+**C5**

cell D6: +**B6**+**C6** *or* +**D2**+**D3**+**D4**+**D5**

We are entering the formula for D6 last since the value of this cell can only be established once formulas are set up for calculating the other margin totals.

Editing Cells

Everyone entering labels and values into cells wants to change them at some point. Perhaps a word was misspelled in a label, a value was entered incorrectly, or you wish to observe the effect of a change. Whatever the reason, 1-2-3 has an EDIT mode to enable you to change cell entries without having to retype them completely. In the EDIT mode new characters keyed in are automatically inserted at the cursor position. If the Delete key is used in the EDIT mode, the character at the cursor position will be deleted. On the IBM PC and similar computers, you enter the EDIT mode by depressing the **F2** function key.

Recalculation Feature

Now it's time to do some experimenting, to explore the power that spreadsheets give to us. Move to cell B2 and change Michaels' sales total from 500 to 600, using the EDIT mode to make the change and the Enter key to enter the new value. Note that not only did the value change in cell B2, but also

cell B6 changed from 850 to 950
cell D2 changed from 700 to 800
and cell D6 changed from 2250 to 2350.

In other words, every cell whose value depended on the value in cell B2 also changed.

You should experiment a bit with this recalculation feature to make sure you understand it. For example, what happens if you change Adams' Region B sales from 100 to 500, or Williams' Region A sales from 50 to −50 (where the negative sign represents the reversal of a previous overcredit to sales)?

It is this automatic recalculation feature that makes electronic spreadsheets so valuable. Most businesses go through an extensive series of "what-if" scenarios when making key decisions. For example, what if sales are 10% lower than expected, or what if the cost of goods sold is $120,000 rather than $100,000? Thus there is a need to constantly recalculate dozens of interdependent figures on schedules to find what the ultimate effect is if something happens. Computations that spreadsheets can do in seconds could take hours to do by hand.

Using 1-2-3 Commands: An Example

When you have finished observing the recalculation feature, restore the worksheet to the form shown in Figure 4-4. Now we'll look at how to use the 1-2-3 command menu to change the width of a worksheet column.

Let's suppose that we want to enter the full names of the agents:

Ted Michaels
Elise Adams
Sam Williams
Terry Jones

Each column on our present worksheet has a (default) width of 9 characters, so if we want to enter the names as shown above, we will need to extend the width of column A. Let's extend the width to 20 characters. To do this, first position the highlight on any cell in column A. This operation is called *pointing,* and we must point to any column whose width we wish to change. Now depress the slash **(/)** key, which will provide the command menu shown in screen 1 of Figure 4-5.

We can select any command from 1-2-3's command menu (or any of the submenus) in one of two ways:

- *Method 1:* Use the **arrow keys** to move the highlight to the desired choice and depress the **Enter** key.
- *Method 2:* Type in the **first letter** of the desired choice. In 1-2-3 each choice on a given menu begins with a unique letter (such as W, R, C, . . . , Q on the command menu). Method 2 is the one many experienced users prefer, as it's much faster and you spend less time looking at the monitor.

Before you select a command, study the command menu for a minute or two. Next, depress the right-arrow key to move the highlight from the "Worksheet" command to the "Range" command. Note that the third line of the control panel also changes, displaying a description of the "Range" command. Depress the right-arrow key again and you'll now observe on the third line of the control panel a description of the "Copy" command.

Now it's time to get back to the business at hand and widen column A. With the cell pointer still in column A and the command menu (screen 1, Figure 4-5) appearing in the control panel, select the

Worksheet

```
A1:
Worksheet  Range  Copy  Move  File  Print  Graph  Data  Quit
Global, Insert, Delete, Column-Width, Erase, Titles, Window, Status
          A          B          C          D          E          F          G ...
1
2
3
.
.
.
```

Highlight is in column A when the command menu is summoned

Screen 1

```
A1:
Global  Insert  Delete  Column-Width  Erase  Titles  Window  Status
Set worksheet settings
          A          B          C          D          E          F          G ...
1
2
3
.
.
.
```

Screen 2

```
A1:
Set  Reset
Set width of current column
          A          B          C          D          E          F          G ...
1
2
3
.
.
.
```

Screen 3

```
A1:
Enter column width (1..72): 20
          A          B          C          D          E          F          G ...
1
2
3
.
.
.
```

Screen 4

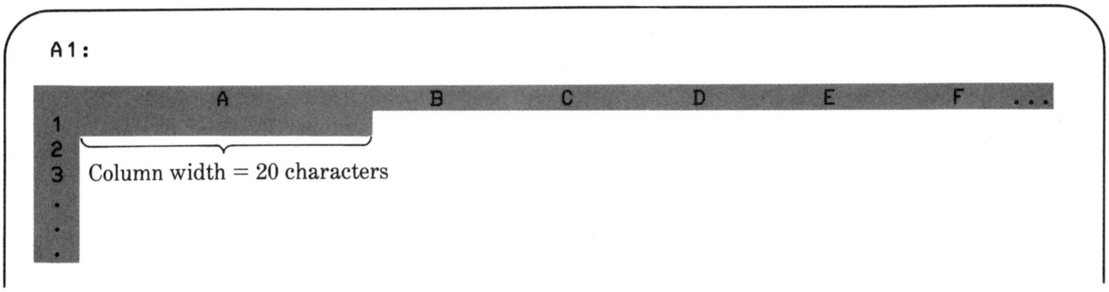

Screen 5

Figure 4-5. (Continued)

command, either by using the **arrow keys** to move the pointer in the control panel back to "Worksheet" and hitting the **Enter** key (method 1) or by typing in **W** (method 2).

When the first submenu appears, select the

Column-width

option (screen 2 in Figure 4-5). Again, this can be done by using either selection method 1 or 2. This option will enable us to change the width of an individual column (the one the cell pointer is pointing to in the worksheet area).

Now (in screen 3), select

Set

indicating that you wish to set the column width.

The next screen to appear (screen 4) is the one where we must enter the new width for column A. Here we type

20 (cr)

Next you'll notice that the menus disappear off the control panel and you get the worksheet shown in screen 5 of Figure 4-5.

Incidentally, there is a shorthand way for describing the sequence of choices we've taken here to change the width of column A:

/ Worksheet Column-width **Set** **20** **(cr)**

We'll be using this notation from now on because it is straightforward and compact.

As mentioned earlier, one of the handy features of 1-2-3 is the ability to use the **Escape** key on the menus. For example, say we are at screen 3 in Figure 4-5 and we suddenly realize that we don't want to change the width of column A. Depressing Escape once will put us back at screen 2; twice, at screen 1, and three times, at the point we were at before hitting the / key. The Escape key is especially useful for beginners, who will be making a lot of wrong choices and would like to experiment freely with the package. Keep in mind that it is not until you enter the final option in a command sequence that the command will actually be invoked.

Saving and Retrieving Worksheets

You can save or retrieve files on disk by again invoking 1-2-3's menus. For example, if you want to save the sales spreadsheet we just worked on you would take the following sequence of actions

/ **F**ile **S**ave

When 1-2-3 responds

NAME OF FILE TO SAVE?

type in the filename under which you want the worksheet (file) saved. Remember that DOS controls disk operations, so that 1-2-3 filenames must also be acceptable DOS filenames. If you decided to name your worksheet EXAMPLE, and wanted to save it on your B-drive disk, you would type

EXAMPLE (cr)

Your worksheet would then be saved under the name

B:EXAMPLE.WKS

As mentioned in Section 2, 1-2-3 always saves worksheets with a .WKS extension. You don't have to explicitly declare this extension when you are preparing worksheets in 1-2-3 because it is automatically assumed. Also, most installed versions of 1-2-3 will automatically default to the B drive when saving or retrieving worksheets. If the version of 1-2-3 on which you are working does not do this, issue the command sequence

/ **F**ile **D**irectory

followed by

B:\ (cr)

to set the default drive to B.

Tomorrow, if you wanted to retrieve the worksheet, you would again set the default drive to B and enter the sequence

/ **F**ile **R**etrieve

When 1-2-3 responds

NAME OF FILE TO RETRIEVE?

type

EXAMPLE (cr)

Again the .WKS extension and B drive are assumed by 1-2-3.

1-2-3 also allows you to save and retrieve files by *pointing* to them. This works as follows: When you issue a save or retrieve command, the .WKS files on the default drive will be displayed in the control panel. To save or retrieve a file, you must *select* it by first using an **arrow key** to move the highlight over the filename and then entering the filename by hitting the **Enter** key.

Printing Worksheets

To print a worksheet it must first be saved. You then invoke the "Print" command from the command menu, as follows

/ **P**rint **P**rinter **R**ange

"Printer" and "Range" are actually selected from the same submenu. We'll be formally introducing the concept of a *range* of cells later but, for now, just type

A1..D6 (cr)

for the range of the sales worksheet. This entry respectively declares the cells in the northwest-most and southeast-most corners of that worksheet. Next, on the same submenu, select

Go

This commands your printer to output your worksheet. Of course, you must have a printer and it must be turned on if this command is to produce the desired effect.

Next, on the same submenu, select

Quit

to leave the command mode. If you want multiple copies of your worksheet, you might want to execute the Go option several more times before leaving the command mode.

Leaving 1-2-3

To leave 1-2-3 and go back to DOS, execute the sequence below:

/ **Q**uit **Y**es **E**xit **Y**es

The first **Y**es will put you back at the Lotus Access System Menu. When you issue the **Q**uit command, the package wants to verify that you really do want to quit and didn't issue this command by accident. When you quit 1-2-3, all *unsaved* materials on your worksheet are unrecoverable. When you invoke the **E**xit option, you must also verify with another **Y**es that you want to go back to DOS.

OTHER USEFUL 1-2-3 OPERATIONS

In addition to the commands you've just learned, there are many other spreadsheet operations that will be useful to you. Among these operations are editing dollar amounts, using functions, moving rapidly around the worksheet, inserting or deleting rows or columns, moving data, copying data, creating separator lines, and using the presentation graphics feature.

Editing Dollar Amounts

Often values in spreadsheets represent dollar amounts. To place characters such as dollar signs, commas, and decimal points into numbers, you must invoke the sequence below:

/ **W**orksheet **G**lobal **F**ormat **C**urrency **2** **(cr)**

Global tells 1-2-3 that you want to take an action that will effect the entire worksheet. **F**ormat enables you to format entries in a certain way. **C**urrency tells 1-2-3 that you want dollar signs, commas (in the appropriate places), and decimal digits in values. Typing in the **2** will edit all values so that they contain 2 digits to the right of the decimal point.

If you get a cell with the contents

****

that means 1-2-3 didn't have enough space in the cell to properly display the formatted number. When this happens, you must enlarge the width of the associated column (as discussed earlier) to see the proper value displayed.

Using 1-2-3 Functions: The Range Concept

1-2-3 has a number of useful functions that can save you a great deal of time in entering formulas. A *function* is a prestored formula. All formulas in 1-2-3 are identified by some *keyword* (such as SUM, AVG, IF, or NPV) and preceded by the @ character. Two of the easiest functions to learn are SUM and AVG.

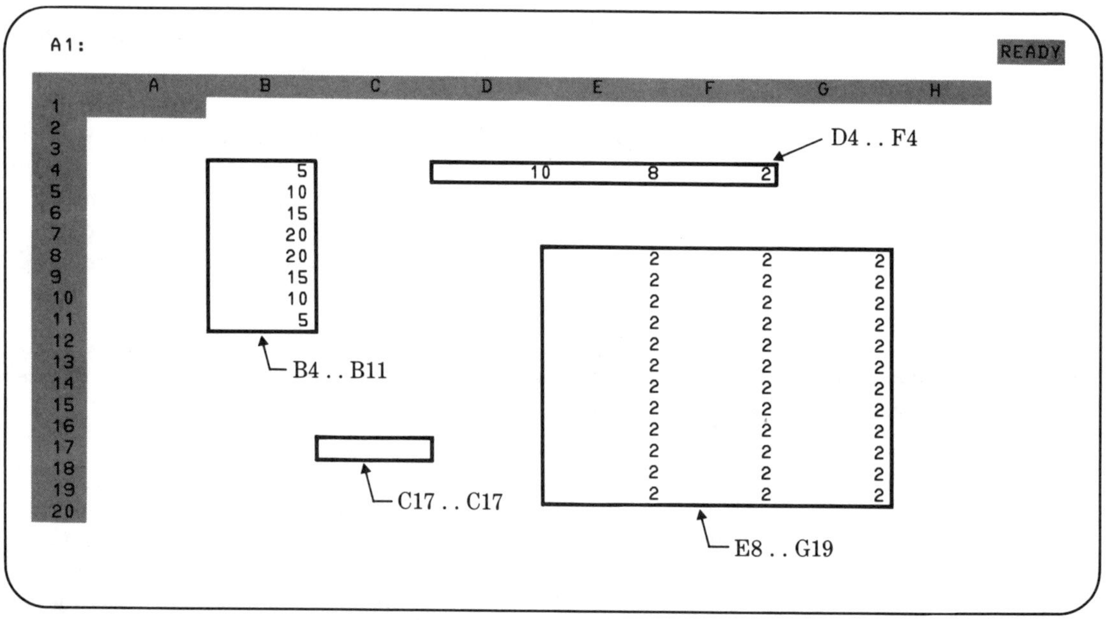

Figure 4-6. The range concept.

To use either of these functions you must first understand the concept of a *range* of cells. The range concept is also useful if you want to print, move, copy, insert, delete, sort, and graph. As you can see, knowing what is meant by a range is absolutely essential if you want to master 1-2-3.

Several examples of ranges are shown in Figure 4-6. A range is defined as one or more cells arranged in a rectangle. It is depicted by declaring the identity of the northwest-most cell, followed by two dots and the identity of the southeast-most cell.

For example, in Figure 4-6, if the current cell is A1 and we type in

@SUM(B4..B11)

the value 100 will be placed in cell A1. Similarly, if we type in **@SUM(D4..F4)** or **@SUM(E8..G19)**, we will get the values 20 or 72, respectively, in cell A1.

The @AVG function works similarly to @SUM. For example, **@AVG(B4..B11)** yields 100/8, or 12.5.

Moving the Highlight Rapidly from One Cell to Another

Everyone preparing a worksheet wants to move to the next cell in the fastest possible way. In many cases the arrow keys are adequate. However, what if you are at cell BX1563 and want to move to cell J206?

One of the most effective ways to move rapidly from one cell to another is by using 1-2-3's GOTO feature. On most computer systems this is implemented with the **F5** function key. When you depress this key, 1-2-3 will prompt you with with the message

Enter address to go to:

At this point you type in the **cell address** (say, J206) you want to move to, depress the **Enter** key, and presto: you're there.

1-2-3 has a number of other cell-movement features that can be handy. For example,

- The **PgUp** key moves you to the same relative cursor position on the previous screen page.
- The **PgDn** key moves you to the same relative cursor position on the next screen page.
- The **Home** key will always move you to cell A1.

Inserting or Deleting Rows or Columns

Inserting and deleting are both done through the "Worksheet" command.

To insert a blank row into the worksheet, point the highlight to the row that will later be below the row you wish to insert. Then, issue the sequence

/ **Worksheet** **Insert** **Row** **(cr)**

If you wish to insert several blank rows, type in any range that covers the rows you wish to insert before you hit the Enter key. Whether you want to insert one or several rows, all rows appearing below the inserted ones are pushed down from their original positions.

If you instead want to insert a blank column, place the highlight on the column that will later appear to the right of the column you wish to insert and enter the sequence

/ **Worksheet** **Insert** **Column** **(cr)**

As with inserting blank rows, you also have the option of entering a range (before the carriage return) if you want to insert more than one blank column.

To delete a row, move the highlight to the row you wish to delete and invoke the sequence

/ **Worksheet** **Delete** **Row** **(cr)**

To delete a column, move the highlight to the column you wish to delete and invoke

/ **Worksheet** **Delete** **Column** **(cr)**

Moving

To physically relocate, that is, move, the contents of one or more cells you must first identify the range of cells to be moved (the *source* range). The concept of a range was discussed earlier. Then you must identify a range (of the same size) where the data is to be relocated (the *target* range).

To learn how to move data, prepare the simple worksheet shown in Figure 4-7*a*. What we'll do is move the data in the range A1..B2 to the range C3..D4, as shown in Figure 4-7*b*. To do this, execute

/ **Move**

1-2-3 will then prompt you with the message

Enter range to move FROM:

Enter this source range as

A1..B2 **(cr)**

1-2-3 will next prompt you with

Enter range to enter TO:

Enter this target range as follows

C3..D4 **(cr)**

At this point, the move you requested should take place on the screen.

There is actually a faster way to move data than the one just described.

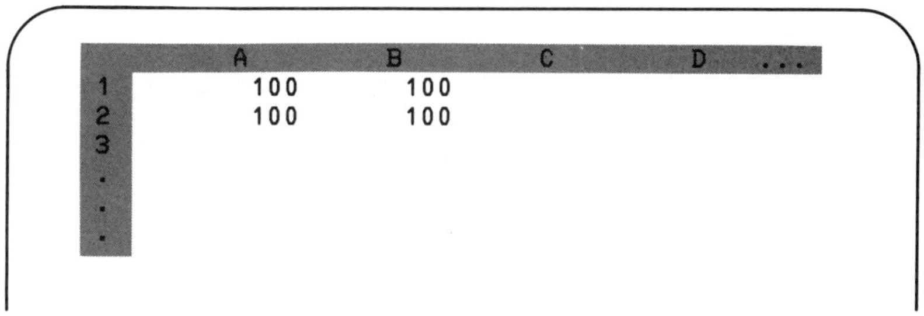

(a) Worksheet *before* move. Data appear in range A1 . . B2.

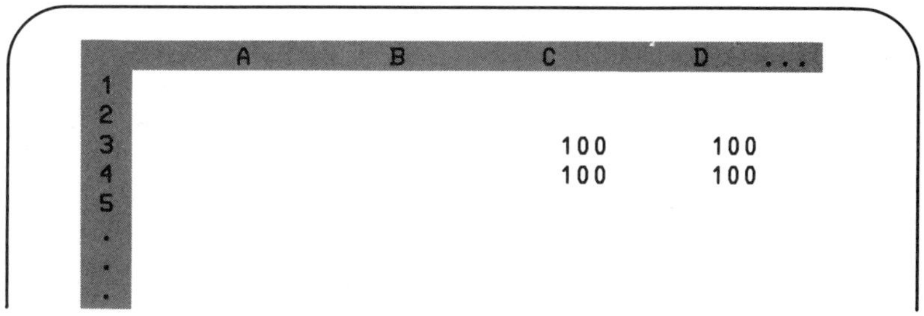

(b) Worksheet *after* move. Data moved from its original locations to range C3 . . D4.

Figure 4-7. Moving the contents of a range of cells.

Rather than typing in both the source and target ranges, you can use 1-2-3's *pointing method* to highlight these range areas on the screen.

To do this, when the prompt

Enter range to move FROM:

appears on the screen, move to cell A1 and hit the period (.). This will "lock in" the northwest-most corner of the source range. Then use the **arrow keys** to move to the southeast-most corner of this range, cell B2. Note that when you get to cell B2 the entire source range has been highlighted, as shown in Figure 4-8. Now, hit the **Enter** key and you'll see the prompt

Enter range to move TO:

As before, use the period (.) to lock in the northwest-most corner of the target range (cell C3), use the **arrow keys** to move to the southeast-most corner (cell D4), and hit the **Enter** key. Presto, you should see your move.

The pointing method works for both moving and copying (discussed next), as well as for printing (discussed earlier).

Copying

To copy the contents of one or more cells into other cells you must, as you did with the "Move" command, identify source and target ranges of cells.

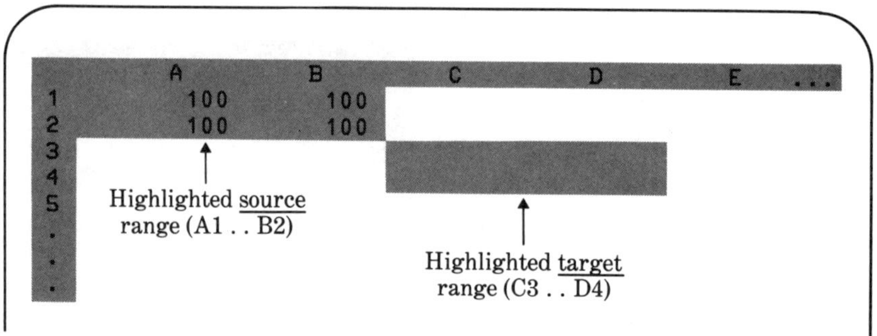

Figure 4-8. Using the pointing method to identify source and target ranges.

Unlike moving, however, copying leaves the copied items in their original locations while replicating them into the new locations.

COPYING CONSTANTS. Items such as numeric constants and labels (which technically are *string constants*) are relatively straightforward to copy. For example, let's go back to Figure 4-7*a* and consider copying (instead of moving) the contents in cells A1..B2 to cells C3..D4. To do this, invoke

/ Copy

From here on in every step you take is virtually identical to those taken when you moved the data. The only difference is in the prompts. For example, instead of the prompt "Enter Range to move FROM:" you'll get the prompt "Enter range to copy FROM:".

COPYING FORMULAS. One of the most useful features of 1-2-3 is its ability to copy formulas. In Chapter 12 we discussed two types of formula replication: *relative replication* and *absolute replication.* Here we'll discuss relative replication first, since it is the most common of the two.

Observe the partially complete worksheet in Figure 4-9. In the first two

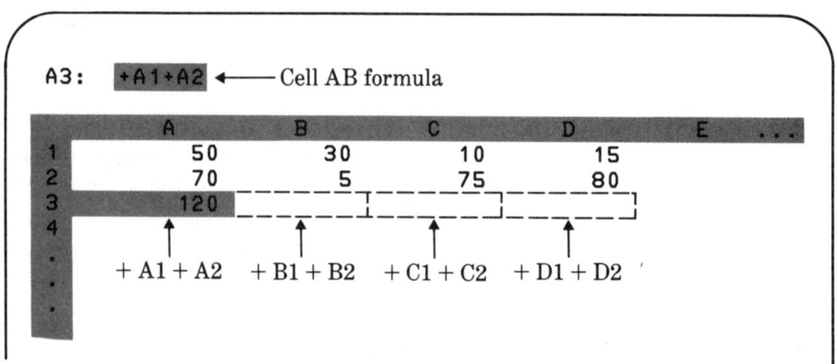

Figure 4-9. Relative copying of formulas.

rows we have numbers that we wish to sum (into row 3). Suppose we've already entered the formula

+A1+A2

for cell A3. What we next need to do is enter the formulas

+B1+B2
+C1+C2
+D1+D2

for cells B3..D3.

Note that these three formulas are almost like the formula in cell A3. The only difference is a *relative* one. That is, each formula is doing the same type of operation, but in different columns. Since this phenomenon is common in accounting and financial calculations, 1-2-3 enables us to handle it without having to type in three new formulas for cells B3, C3, and D3.

What we want to tell 1-2-3 is to replicate the formula in cell A1 to these three cells in a relative way. Since relative replication is the most common type of copy operation, 1-2-3 automatically defaults to it. In other words, whenever we copy a cell with a formula assigned to it, 1-2-3 assumes we are doing relative replication.

Once you understand these things, everything else is just as if copying constants. Issue the sequence

/ Copy

When 1-2-3 responds

Range of cells to copy FROM:

move the cell pointer to cell A3 and hit the **Enter** key. Next, when 1-2-3 responds

Range of cells to copy TO:

you can use the pointer method, as before, to highlight and enter this range:

B3..D3 (cr)

Upon hitting the Enter key, you should notice the proper sums—35, 85, and 95—in cells B3, C3, and D3 respectively.

In some cases we might not want formulas to be copied in a relative way. Suppose for example, in Figure 4-9, that we wanted the formula +A1+A2 copied exactly as is into cells B3, C3, and D3. In other words, these three cells are each to contain +A1+A2. Copying a formula in this way is known as *absolute* replication.

To perform such a COPY operation, go back to cell A3, enter the EDIT mode, and rewrite the formula as

+**A1**+**A2** **(cr)**

Then copy this formula into the other cells—B3, C3, and D3—in the usual way.

Creating Separator Lines

Business reports often make use of separator lines to neatly separate titles, related rows, or column footings from other data. A separator line is shown in Figure 4-10*b*, separating the column footings from the rest of the worksheet.

Let's create this separator line, assuming that we're starting out with the worksheet in Figure 4-10*a*. First, put the highlight on a cell in row 3 and execute the sequence

/ **W**orksheet **I**nsert **R**ow **(cr)**

This will create a blank row where we want the separator line to appear and move the original row 3 down one row.

To create the separator line itself, move to cell A3 and issue the three-keystroke sequence below

\ – **(cr)**

The backward slash (\) is a *repeat character* that, in this case, tells 1-2-3 that you want cell A3 filled entirely with hyphens. Once this is done, all you need to do to create the separator line is to copy this 9-hyphen *label* into cells B3..D3. This can be done in the usual manner by invoking the "Copy" command, identifying cell A3..A3 as the source range, and identifying cells B3..D3 as the target range.

	A	B	C	D	E ...
1	50	30	10	15	
2	70	5	75	80	
3	120	35	85	95	
4					
5					
.					
.					
.					

(a) Worksheet before separator line is created.

	A	B	C	D	E ...
1	50	30	10	15	
2	70	5	75	80	
3	---------	---------	---------	---------	
4	120	35	85	95	
5					
.					
.					
.					

(b) Worksheet after separator line is created.

Figure 4-10. Using a separator line.

Presentation Graphics

It's a well-known fact that people can assimilate information faster if it's presented to them in picture form. So it's not surprising that one of 1-2-3's most popular features is its ability to rapidly develop presentation-quality graphs from spreadsheet data. Here we'll explain how to use 1-2-3 to construct, save, and print a bar chart, pie chart, and line chart (see Figures 4-11 through 4-13 for examples of each of these types of graphs).

Before we begin, you should make sure that your monitor is capable of displaying graphics and that your system unit has a *graphics display board.* Most monitors sold for the IBM PC and similar computers are capable of producing graphics. However, unless your system unit has a graphics display board, you will not be able to see any graphs on your display screen. Many dot-matrix printers made today support graphics output, but you should check to see that your printer does before proceeding.

BAR CHARTS. To see how to construct a bar chart, we'll use the data appearing in the sales worksheet of Figure 4-4. The result of our actions will be the graph shown in Figure 4-11.

To begin, retrieve the worksheet in Figure 4-4 so it appears on your monitor screen. Then invoke

/ **G**raph **T**ype **B**ar

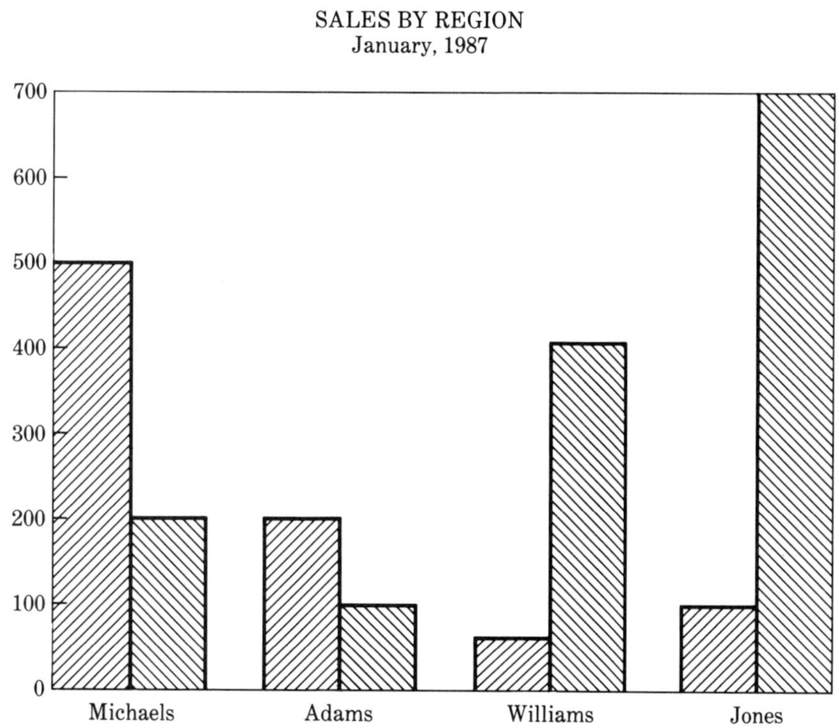

Figure 4-11. A bar chart.

What you've done is the following. The **G**raph command tells 1-2-3 that you want to graph the worksheet that's currently on the screen. In response, 1-2-3 will provide the *graph submenu* that you see below:

Type X A B C D E F Reset View Save Options Name Quit

The **T**ype command on this submenu summons the *type submenu*, shown below

Line Bar XY Stacked-Bar Pie

which enables you to choose the type of graph you want. **B**ar is chosen from this submenu because, as you've probably already guessed, we want a bar chart.

Now it's time to select the worksheet data that are to be graphed and to tell 1-2-3 where these data are to appear in the graph. To place the names of the sales agents along the graph's X-axis, select

X

from the graph submenu. When the computer responds

Enter X-axis range:

either type in

A2..A5 (cr)

or use the pointing method described on page 57 to declare the range. When this is accomplished, you'll be returned to the graph submenu. Now select

A

to identify the data that will be used to graph the leftmost bar for each sales agent in Figure 4-11. These data appear in column B of the worksheet. When the computer responds

Enter first data range:

you again either type in the range or point to it on the screen.

When you are returned to the graph submenu, select

B

and enter the "second data range" (used to construct the rightmost bars for each agent in the chart) in the same way you entered the A range. The B-range data appear in column C of the worksheet. Once this is done, you'll again be returned to the graph submenu.

At this point the graph is finished, except for the title. You can title the graph by selecting

Options

on the graph submenu. 1-2-3 lets you supply titles of up to two lines. By selecting

First

and typing

SALES BY REGION (cr)

after the prompt, you'll produce the first line of the title of the graph in Figure 4-11. By selecting

Second

and typing

January, 1987 (cr)

after the prompt, you'll produce the second line.

Now the graph is completed and it's time to look at it on the screen. To do this, first select

Quit

to backtrack to the graph submenu. Then select

View

At this point your graph should appear on the screen.

If you wish to change the graph for any reason, reselect any of the graph-command options discussed so far and make the appropriate changes. As usual, you can either type your changes or use the pointer method to make them.

When your graph is satisfactory, select

Save

from the graph submenu to output the graph onto disk. In answer to the prompt asking for a filename to save to, supply a name of 1 to 8 characters. 1-2-3 automatically adds the extension .PIC to all saved graphs.

To print any 1-2-3 graph, you first need to return to the Lotus Access System Menu (see page 53, "Leaving 1-2-3"). Instead of exiting to DOS, select

PrintGraph

1-2-3 will respond with the message*

Insert Lotus PrintGraph disk in Drive A
and press [Enter]; press [Esc] to quit

Follow the directions and press the **Enter** key. The main menu of the PrintGraph disk will be pointing to

Select

which you should select. The next screen to appear lists the names of graphs that are saved on the B drive (i.e., those graphs with .PIC extensions). A highlight appears over the topmost name. Using the **down-arrow key**

*1-2-3 uses a special disk, called the PrintGraph disk, to enable you to output graphs onto paper. This disk is automatically supplied with every copy of 1-2-3 sold.

you can move this highlight to any of the names on the list. As usual, you select the highlighted entry by depressing the **Enter** key.

Once you've selected the graph to be printed, you'll be returned to the main PrintGraph menu. At this point, first make sure your printer is activated and then select

Go

to print your graph. Most printers take a few minutes or so to print a single graph, so be patient.

PIE CHARTS. Pie charts are constructed in a manner very similar to bar charts.

To produce the pie chart in Figure 4-12, again summon the worksheet of Figure 4-4 to your screen and issue the sequence

/ **Graph** **Type** **Pie**

The procedure to identify the X range and the two-line title for the graph is identical to the corresponding process for bar charts. You should identify the A range as cells D2..D5. There is no B range. As with bar charts, you would issue the View command to display the pie chart, issue the Save command to save the chart, and use the PrintGraph disk for printer output.

LINE CHARTS. The procedure for constructing line charts, once you understand how to make bar and pie charts, is a snap.

Suppose, for example, that the sales (in units) for a new product in a particular five-week period are as follows: 25 units for the first week, 45

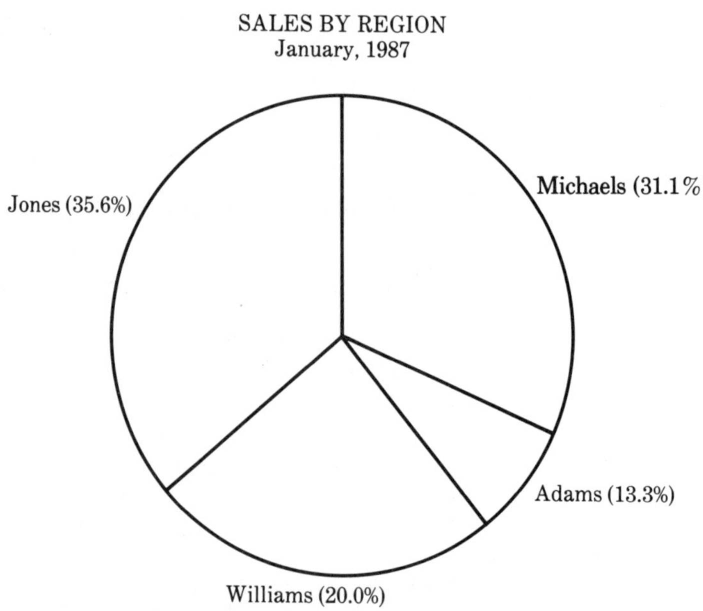

Figure 4-12. A pie chart.

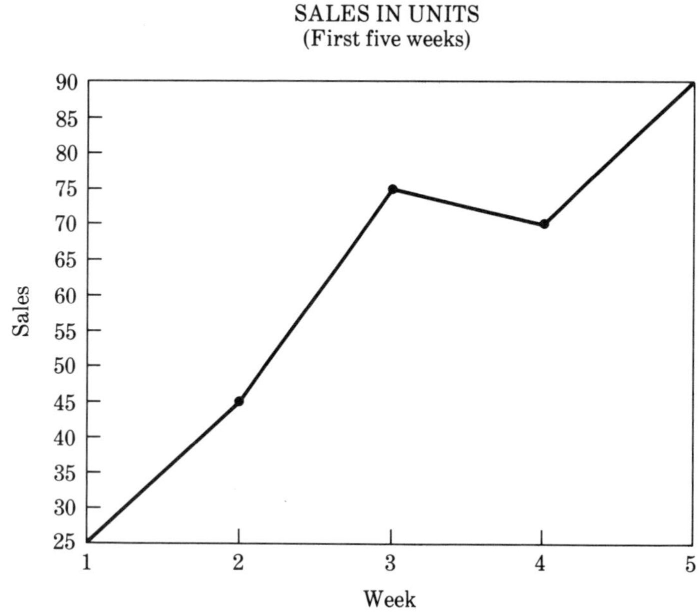

Figure 4-13. A line chart.

units for the second week, 75 units for the third week, 70 units for the fourth week, and 90 units for the fifth week. Here's how you can create the line chart shown in Figure 4-13. Enter these data into a new worksheet so that cells A1, A2, A3, A4, and A5 respectively contain 1, 2, 3, 4, and 5 and cells B1, B2, B3, B4, and B5 respectively contain 25, 45, 75, 70, and 90. Then issue the sequence

/ **Graph** **Type** **Line**

When you return to the graph submenu, identify the X range as A1..A5 and the A range as B1..B5. Then type in the two-line title

SALES IN UNITS
(First five weeks)

in a manner similar to the one for bar charts.

To label the X-axis from the graph submenu, execute the sequence

Options **T**itles **X**-axis

When 1-2-3 prompts with

Enter X-axis title:

type

Week (cr)

To label the Y-axis from the graph submenu, execute the sequence

Options **T**itles **Y**-axis

When 1-2-3 prompts with

Enter Y-axis title:

type

Sales (cr)

At this point, the graph is finished and all actions you take to view it, save it, and print it are identical to those for bar charts and line charts.

Exercises

1. Prepare the worksheet below:

	A	B	C	D	E	...
1	Day	Jan 1	Jan 2	Jan 3		
2	Sales	500	800	600		
3	Costs	350	700	150		
4	Profits	150	100	450		
.						
.						
.						

(*Note:* Profits are calculated as Sales less Costs.) When you've finished, save the worksheet. Next, leave 1-2-3 and enter DOS. Then, return to 1-2-3 and retrieve the worksheet. Finally, output the worksheet on your printer.

2. Adjust the column widths in Exercise 1 as follows:

Column A: 20 characters
Column B: 6 characters
Column C: 6 characters
Column D: 6 characters

3. Use the @SUM function to sum up the numbers in cells A1..A5 below. Place this sum in cell A6.

	A	...
1	25	
2	15	
3	32	
4	18	
5	19	
.		
.		
.		

4. Redo Exercise 1, formatting sales and costs as follows:

	Jan 1	Jan 2	Jan 3
Sales	$500,000.00	$800,000.00	$600,000.00
Costs	$350,000.00	$700,000.00	$150,000.00
Profits	$150,000.00	$100,000.00	$450,000.00

(*Note:* You'll first need to extend the widths of the columns that will contain the dollar amounts.)

5. Calculate the average sales, costs, and profits for the 3 days shown in Exercise 4, placing these values into a 5th column on your worksheet. How would your worksheet change if the January 1 costs were actually $50,000 instead of $350,000 . . . or if January 3 sales were $90,000 instead of $600,000?
6. Prepare the worksheet below, using the "Copy" command to copy the relative formula in cell B4 to cells C4, D4, and E4. (*Note:* Income is Revenue less Expenses.)

	A	B	C	D	E	F	. . .
1	Quarter	1st	2nd	3rd	4th		
2	Revenue	$200	$100	$600	$200		
3	Expenses	$130	$50	$100	$300		
4	Income	$70	$50	$500	($100)		
.							
.							
.							

7. Use the "Move" command to move the worksheet in Exercise 6 to the range of cells L7..P10.
8. Create separator lines on the worksheet of Exercise 6, as shown below.

	A	B	C	D	E	F	. . .
1	Quarter	1st	2nd	3rd	4th		
2	----------	----------	----------	----------	----------		
3	Revenue	$200	$100	$600	$200		
4	Expenses	$130	$50	$100	$300		
5		----------	----------	----------	----------		
6	Income	$70	$50	$500	($100)		
.							
.							
.							

9. Using data from Figure 4-4 (page 46) construct two pie charts: one for Region A, showing the percentage of sales attributable to each of the four sales agents, and one for Region B, also showing the percentage of sales attributable to each of the four sales agents.

Section 5

dBASE II and III

One can hardly discuss microcomputer-based database management systems without some mention of dBASE II and III, which, at this writing, account for over 50% of that market. dBASE II, introduced on 8-bit, CP/M-based microcomputers in 1981, was one of the earliest database management systems for microcomputers, as well as one of the most popular. With the introduction of the 16-bit IBM PC and the PC-DOS operating system in 1983, dBASE II was made available for these more powerful computer systems.

In 1984 dBASE's vendor, Ashton-Tate, introduced dBASE III. Although Ashton-Tate does not consider dBASE III an upgrade of dBASE II, the two packages are very similar in both their command structures and their approaches to data management. Any differences will, of course, be called to your attention in this *Guide* where appropriate.

In December, 1985 Ashton-Tate released dBASE III Plus, which contains several features not found in dBASE III. These include the ability to run on local area networks, a new pull-down menu interface, and a number of new commands. In this *Guide,* all references made to dBASE III also apply to dBASE III Plus.

WHAT dBASE DOES

Both dBASE II and dBASE III are relational database management systems. Although they lack the sophistication of many larger database systems, they enable you to establish several files of data and, if you wish, to *relate* data between files in order to make queries and create reports. Both dBASE II and III are equipped with a structured, high-level programming language that enables you to handle file data as you would with languages such as BASIC or COBOL. You can also effectively use dBASE commands without writing programs, as will be shown in this *Guide.*

As discussed in detail in Chapter 13 of *Understanding Computers and Data Processing,* the capability of relating data between "logical" files is the feature that separates *database management systems* from data management packages called *file managers.* File managers can only manipulate data from one file at a time. These differences notwithstanding, database management systems and file managers serve the same purpose. They enable you to store large volumes of data and have easy, flexible access to them.

So you can fully grasp what dBASE is capable of doing, let's look at a simple example. Refer to Figure 5-1. Figure 5-1*a* shows data on five

CUSTNUM	NAME	STREET	CITY	STATE	ZIP	CHARGE
810	John T. Smith	31 Cedarcrest	Boulder	CO	80302	.T.
775	Sally Jones	725 Agua Fria	Santa Fe	NM	87501	.T.
690	William Holmes	3269 Fast Lane	Santa Fe	NM	87501	.F.
840	Artis Smith	2332 Alameda	Lakewood	CO	80215	.T.
574	Nellie Deutsch	23 E. Spruce	Olathe	KS	66061	.F.

(a) CUSTOMER file.

PRODNUM	DESCRIP	PRICE
001	Nordic hat	10.00
002	Nylon windpants	40.00
003	Thermal ski socks	7.00
004	Indy Jones jacket, large	90.00
005	Rozelle headband	6.00

(b) PRODUCT file.

ORDNUM	CUSTNUM	DATE
001	775	2/3/87
002	775	2/5/87
003	810	2/7/87
004	574	2/16/87
005	810	2/16/87
006	810	2/18/87

(c) ORDER file.

ORDNUM	QTY	PRODNUM
001	2	003
001	1	002
002	1	001
003	1	001
003	3	003
004	1	001
004	1	002
004	1	003
005	2	003
006	1	004
006	1	005

(d) ODETAILS file.

Figure 5-1. Avalanche Outfitter's four data files.

customers of Avalanche Outfitters, a mail-order firm. Each type of data is known as a *field.* Thus there's a customer-number field (CUSTNUM), a name field (NAME), a street-address field (STREET), and so forth. The data collected on each person forms a *record.* As you can see, there are five records in Figure 5-1*a*, with each record consisting of seven fields. Collectively the five records comprise a *file.* In dBASE, a file is also called a *database,* although in many other database management environments these two terms are not synonymous.

Both dBASE II and III require you to provide a name for each field and a name for each file. For example, we've called the entire customer file CUSTOMER, and the customer-number field of this file, CUSTNUM. Notice that these names conform to DOS's naming conventions. The size limitations on fields, records, and files are provided in Figure 5-2. In dBASE, we can create as many files as we wish to, although there are limitations on the number of files that can be *active* (i.e. in use) at once.

To see how dBASE can handle file data and relate data between them consider also the files in Figures 5-1*b*, 5-1*c*, and 5-1*d*. Here, we have a product file (PRODUCT), consisting of product descriptions and prices; an order file (ORDER), consisting of individual orders placed by customers (who are in the customer file); and a file showing some of the details of each order (ODETAILS). The ODETAILS file shows how many units of each product (of the product file) were shipped on each order (of the order file). You should note that the files in Figures 5-1*b*, 5-1*c*, and 5-1*d* respectively contain 5, 6, and 11 records, all consisting of 3 fields.

Each of these files, by themselves, can provide a wealth of useful information. For example, we can tap the CUSTOMER file for a listing of all customers from Colorado. Or, we can use that same file to prepare mailing labels for catalogs that are to be sent out next month.

You may also have guessed that Avalanche Outfitters may want to *relate* data appearing in different files. For example, if you've ever ordered anything through the mail, you've probably received an invoice such as the one in Figure 5-3. Note that this invoice contains data from several files. When the order is placed, separate records are created in Avalanche's ORDER and ODETAIL files. To produce the invoice, name and shipping addresses are extracted from the CUSTOMER file, prices and descriptions are extracted from the PRODUCT file, the date is taken from the ORDER file, and the quantities ordered are taken from the ODETAILS file. The computational facilities of the database system then produce the totals in the last column. Thus, through the power of database technology, an invoice can be prepared quickly, with minimum error.

There are a number of other reasons we may want to relate data appearing in different files. Avalanche's management may want the names of all customers who have ordered more than $1000 worth of merchandise during 1987. Or, an angry customer might call saying she ordered a Nordic hat rather than a large Indy Jones jacket, requiring Avalanche personnel to reconstruct the original order.

Most of the examples you'll see in this *Guide* involve working on only one file at a time. In fact, many of the data management problems you'll probably face in your lifetime will be simple enough not to involve relating data between files. Nonetheless, the ability to relate data between files is a

	dBASE II	dBASE III
Fields per record	32	128
Records per file	65,535	1,000,000,000
Characters per record	1,000	4,000
Active data files	2	10

Figure 5-2. Constraints on sizes of dBASE fields, records, and files.

relatively common application and it is what database management systems are all about, so we've included an example later in the *Guide* to show you how dBASE can work with multiple files. Besides, even though you may not need to relate data yourself, you'll be interfacing with a lot of database management systems in the real world—from the mail-order firms that sell you clothes to the taxing agencies that use your social security number to relate files of data on your interest-bearing financial transactions. You should at least be familiar with how these systems work.

HOW dBASE WORKS

To do anything useful in dBASE you must learn two things: how to *define* data and how to *manipulate* data.

```
                Order number:  001
                Date placed:  2/3/87
                Ship to:  Sally Jones
                          725 Agua Fria
                          Santa Fe, NM 87501


Quantity        Description            Unit price        Total price
--------        -----------            ----------        -----------
    2           Thermal ski socks         7.00             $ 14.00
    1           Nylon windpants          40.00               40.00
                                                           -------
                                                           $ 54.00


                Remit check to:  AVALANCHE OUTFITTERS
                                 P.O. Box 8000
                                 Boulder, Colorado 80302
```

Figure 5-3. An invoice prepared from a relational database system (with data from the four files of Figure 5-1).

Data Definition

In Figure 5-1 we looked at four files. The process of describing to dBASE the physical characteristics of each of these files—how many fields they have, the names of each field, and so forth—is called *data definition.*

For example, let's look at the file in Figure 5-1*b*. We could describe the physical characteristics, or *structure,* of this file as follows:

Filename: **PRODUCT**

Field	Field Name	Field Type	Field Width	Decimal
1	**PRODNUM**	**C**	**3**	
2	**DESCRIP**	**C**	**25**	
3	**PRICE**	**N**	**6**	**2**

(Later we'll show exactly how you would enter such data with dBASE.) In both dBASE II and III we are *prompted* for structure data, so only the entries that are boldfaced represent data that you'll be typing in.

As you can see, we first provide dBASE with the name of the file. Then we describe the characteristics of each field. For example, we've told dBASE that the first field is named PRODNUM. It will consist of *character* (C) *data* that is at most 3 characters in length. Character data is data that consists of text that will not be manipulated mathematically. dBASE can also handle numeric data, upon which we can perform arithmetic operations. For example, field 3 (PRICE) consists of *numeric* (N) *data* that is at most 6 characters in length and will have 2 digits beyond the decimal point (which is included in the 6-character length).

The C and N characters of the structure just defined are called *field descriptors.* Among the several field descriptors that are available in dBASE are the three shown in Figure 5-4. The *logical* (L) *data* field descriptor, which we haven't yet discussed, has either the value true (T) or false (F). In the customer file, the CHARGE field uses this descriptor to distinguish charge from cash customers.

The **CREATE** command, which you'll shortly learn about, is used to define a file's structure to dBASE.

Data Manipulation

After you've described the structure of a file to dBASE, you'll want to enter records into the file and do useful things with these records. For example, at

Field Type	Identifier	Maximum Data Length
Character data	C	24 characters
Numeric data	N	19 characters
Logical data	L	1 character

Figure 5-4. Three dBASE field descriptors.

some point you'll probably want to add, delete, or modify records. And, maybe you'll want a listing on your printer of certain records in a particular file—say, in the order of original entry or in sorted order. And, as you saw with Avalanche Outfitters, maybe you'll want to relate files to produce invoices or informative reports. Whatever the case, the process of doing anything at all to the files whose structures you've previously defined to dBASE is called *data manipulation.*

To manipulate file data in any way, dBASE insists that you first make the file "active." This is done through the **USE** command. Before you can execute other data manipulation commands on a file, you must *point* to the file with this command.

As we get into dBASE, keep in mind that there are commands for both data definition and data manipulation operations. If the only programming language you're familiar with is BASIC, chances are you've only manipulated data. Most versions of BASIC do not have a "visible" data definition facility. On the other hand, if you've worked with Pascal or COBOL, you're probably already very familiar with both data definition and data manipulation. Each of these languages require their programs to contain specific and distinct sections (or divisions) where data is defined and where data is manipulated.

To keep things relatively simple, we'll only consider using dBASE commands interactively in the *Guide,* one at a time. Keep in mind, however that you could also batch a sequence of dBASE commands in a file, save the file on disk, and execute the file as you would a regular computer program.

GETTING STARTED: YOUR FIRST dBASE EXERCISES

Now that you've seen how dBASE is set up to work, let's use it to do a few simple exercises. In this subsection we'll look at how to

- Invoke dBASE from DOS.
- Describe the structure of a file to dBASE.
- Open and close a file. (*Note:* Opening a file makes it active; closing a file deactivates it.)
- Add records to a file.
- List the records that comprise a file—both on your display screen and on your printer.
- Delete records from a file.
- Edit (that is, modify) records in a file.
- Extract records with specific characteristics from a file.
- Quit a dBASE session and get back to DOS.

In the next subsection, you'll learn about some advanced dBASE operations: sorting files, relating data from two databases, and preparing reports.

Invoking dBASE

To get started with dBASE, boot up your computer with DOS in the usual way. When the A> prompt appears, put your dBASE program disk into the A drive and the formatted disk that will contain your dBASE files into the B drive. Then, type

A>**DBASE** **(cr)**

After a moment's pause, some versions of dBASE will ask you to supply the current date. If this is the case, type in today's date and press the **Enter** key. For example,

10/15/87 **(cr)**

Next you'll see dBASE's dot prompt (.), which is your signal to type in a dBASE command. dBASE will display this prompt whenever it's time for you to enter a command. For the sake of clarity, the *Guide* will often show both the dot prompt and the command (in boldface) that you must respond with. It's important to keep in mind, however, that you never type the dot—the computer system supplies it for you.

Defining Data: The CREATE Command

Now that you have entered dBASE, it's time to define your first dBASE file. As mentioned earlier, we must describe to dBASE each field of the records that will later be put into a file. Also, we must provide a name for each field and a name for the entire file. At the dot prompt, type in (but not the dot)

.**CREATE B:CUSTOMER** **(cr)**

What we will be doing here is describing the CUSTOMER file that was shown in Figure 5-1*a*. The B before the filename tells dBASE that we want this file created on the B drive. Alternatively, you can issue the command

.**SET DEFAULT TO B:** **(cr)**

to establish the B drive as the default drive, before you issue the CREATE command. If you choose to do this, follow the SET DEFAULT TO command above with

.**CREATE CUSTOMER** **(cr)**

We'll assume in the text that follows that the default drive is B.

Once you have issued the CREATE command above you'll be prompted for the structure of CUSTOMER, and you must describe this file in a manner resembling what you saw earlier for the PRODUCT file (refer to page 72). dBASE II and III differ in the way this structure is to be entered.

dBASE II. In dBASE II, you'll get a screen similar to the one in Figure 5-5*a*. You enter data as shown in Figure 5-5*b*. Note that all of the data you enter (which is highlighted)—field name, field type, etc.—are separated by commas. The depression of the **Enter** key, where appropriate, is also shown in the figure.

dBASE III. In dBASE III, invoking the CREATE command provides a fresh screen, similar to the one in Figure 5-5*c*. The highlighted entries in Figure 5-5*d* represent the data you must supply each time the screen cursor in Figure 5-5*c* advances to the next field.

As you key in each "field name" you must hit the **Enter** key to enter it. As you key in each field "type" you follow the procedure below:

- Hit the **C** key (or **Enter** key) if the field type is Character.
- Hit the **N** key if the field type is Numeric.
- Hit the **L** key if the field type is Logical.

Note that the *character* field type ("Char/text") is the *default* type and always appears before you strike a key. No matter which of these keys you strike, dBASE advances the screen cursor to where you describe the next piece of structure data—the field width. Here, you **type in a field width,** followed by hitting the **Enter** key. If you enter a field "type" of *numeric,*

```
. CREATE CUSTOMER  (cr)
ENTER RECORD STRUCTURE AS FOLLOWS:
 FIELD   NAME,TYPE,WIDTH,DECIMAL PLACES
 001
```

(a)

```
. CREATE CUSTOMER  (cr)
ENTER RECORD STRUCTURE AS FOLLOWS:
 FIELD   NAME,TYPE,WIDTH,DECIMAL PLACES
 001     CUSTNUM,C,3  (cr)
 002     NAME,C,15  (cr)
 003     STREET,C,15  (cr)
 004     CITY,C,10  (cr)
 005     STATE,C,2  (cr)
 006     ZIP,C,5  (cr)
 007     CHARGE,L,1  (cr)
 008     (cr)
INPUT DATA NOW? N  (cr)
```

(b)

Figure 5-5. Using the CREATE command to define the file structure for the CUSTOMER file.

you'll next be asked to supply the number of digits to the right of the decimal point ("Dec"); otherwise, you'll automatically be advanced to the next field name.

In both dBASE II and III, when you are finished describing all of the fields, you depress the **Enter** key when asked to supply the description for another field (as shown in Figures 5-5*b* and 5-5*d*). At this point the prompt

INPUT DATA NOW?

will appear. dBASE lets you put records into a file as soon as you have completely defined it—by typing **Y** to this prompt. However, we'll choose to put records into the file by issuing another dBASE command. So, type

N (cr)

indicating that you don't want to place records into the file now. Now the dot prompt will appear, signalling that dBASE awaits your next command.

Incidentally, when you use the CREATE command to set up a file, dBASE will allocate space on disk for this file and record its name in your disk's directory (with a .DBF extension). Hence, the file you've just defined will be named

CUSTOMER.DBF

on your disk. And, of course, you'll refer to it in dBASE as

CUSTOMER

if your default drive is B. With dBASE you don't have to worry about saving a file's structure or the records you later put into the file—dBASE automatically does these things for you!

If at some later point you want to see the structure you've just defined on your monitor screen, issue the command

.DISPLAY STRUCTURE (cr)

If a structure is unsuitable, you can change it with the command

.MODIFY STRUCTURE (cr)

If you use the MODIFY STRUCTURE command, follow the directions dBASE supplies on the screen. Most importantly, if the file you are restructuring already has data, make sure these data can fit into the new field descriptions.

Opening and Closing a dBASE File: The USE Command

Once you've described a file to dBASE you must always *open* the file if you want to work with it in any way. Opening a file makes it active for

```
B:CUSTOMER.dbf


    field name   type      width       dec

1   [cursor]     Char/text
         ↑
    Screen cursor
```

(c)

```
B:CUSTOMER.dbf


    field name   type      width       dec

1   CUSTNUM(cr)  Char/text (cr)     3   (cr)
2   NAME(cr)     Char/text (cr)    15   (cr)
3   STREET(cr)   Char/text (cr)    15   (cr)
4   CITY(cr)     Char/text (cr)    10   (cr)
5   STATE(cr)    Char/text (cr)     2   (cr)
6   ZIP(cr)      Char/text (cr)     5   (cr)
7   CHARGE(cr)   Logical (cr)       1   (cr)
8   (cr)

INPUT DATA NOW?  N  (cr)
```

(d)

Figure 5-5. (continued)

processing. Thus if you want to add records, delete records, modify records, print all or any portion of the file, sort the file, prepare reports with the file, and so forth, you must first instruct dBASE to open the file. This is done with the USE command.

For example, to open the CUSTOMER file, type

.USE CUSTOMER (cr)

What dBASE will do first in response to this command is ascertain that the file exists. This entails checking to see if CUSTOMER.DBF is listed in the directory of the disk in the B drive. Assuming the file does exist, dBASE then points to the first record position of the file.

The USE command can also be employed to *close* a file. Once a file is closed, you'll no longer have access to it unless you open it again. To close the CUSTOMER file when you are currently pointing to it, issue

.USE (cr)

Although closing a file normally isn't necessary, it'll free up the space that the file is occupying in main memory.

Placing Records into a File: The APPEND Command

The APPEND command is used to place records into a file. Thus once you've employed the USE command to open the file, and you have your next dot prompt, issue the command

.APPEND (cr)

This command tells dBASE that you want to add records to the end of a file. If there are no records in the file, the APPEND command automatically points you to the first record position. On the other hand, if there are already 15 records in the file, APPEND will point to the 16th record position.

Since at this time there are no records in the file, you'll get a screen similar to the one shown in Figure 5-6*a*, if you are using dBASE II; or the one shown in Figure 5-6*c*, if you are in dBASE III. At this point you respond as shown in Figure 5-6*b* if you are a dBASE II user, or as shown in Figure 5-6*d* if you are a dBASE III user. In each case, you must hit the **Enter** key if the data you're entering does not completely fill up the field width. If the data does fill the field width, dBASE automatically advances you to the next field.

When you have entered data for the last field in a record, dBASE will automatically supply you a fresh "form" to fill in the data for the next record. If you have no more records to add, hit the **Enter** key again, to get back to the dot prompt.

Listing Records in a File: The LIST Command

Once you have set up a file of records you'll probably want to display or print the records to inspect their contents. If you wish to display the file on your monitor screen, issue the command

.LIST (cr)

This will produce a listing somewhat like the one shown in Figure 5-7*a*. If, instead, you wish to direct the listing to your printer, issue the sequence of commands shown in Figure 5-7*b* to activate (and later deactivate) the printer. While the SET PRINT ON command is active, everything you type

```
RECORD #  00001
CUSTNUM     :   :
NAME        :                    :
STREET      :                    :
CITY        :              :
STATE       :  :
ZIP         :      :
CHARGE      : :
```

(a) A blank dBASE II form

```
RECORD #  00001
CUSTNUM     :001:
NAME        :John T. Smith   :  (cr needed)
STREET      :31 Cedarcrest   :  (cr needed)
CITY        :Boulder     :  (cr needed)
STATE       :CO:
ZIP         :80302:
CHARGE      :T:
```

(b) A filled-in dBASE II form

```
RECORD No.
CUSTNUM
NAME
STREET
CITY
STATE
ZIP
CHARGE
```

(c) A blank dBASE III form

```
RECORD No.       1
CUSTNUM      810
NAME         John T. Smith      (cr needed)
STREET       31 Cedarcrest      (cr needed)
CITY         Boulder        (cr needed)
STATE        CO
ZIP          80302
CHARGE       T
```

(d) A filled-in dBASE III form

Figure 5-6. APPENDing records to a file.

```
. LIST  (cr)
Record#  CUSTNUM NAME             STREET          CITY        STATE ZIP    CHARGE
      1  810     John T. Smith    31 Cedarcrest   Boulder     CO    80302  .T.
      2  775     Sally Jones      725 Agua Fria   Santa Fe    NM    87501  .T.
      3  690     William Holmes   3269 Fast Lane  Santa Fe    NM    87501  .T.
      4  840     Artis Smith      2332 Alameda    Lakewood    CO    80215  .T.
      5  574     Nellie Deutsch   23 E. Spruce    Olathe      KS    66061  .F.
```

(a) Outputting the list on the monitor screen

```
. SET PRINT ON  (cr)
. LIST  (cr)
Record#  CUSTNUM NAME             STREET          CITY        STATE ZIP    CHARGE
      1  810     John T. Smith    31 Cedarcrest   Boulder     CO    80302  .T..
      2  775     Sally Jones      725 Agua Fria   Santa Fe    NM    87501  .T.
      3  690     William Holmes   3269 Fast Lane  Santa Fe    NM    87501  .T.
      4  840     Artis Smith      2332 Alameda    Lakewood    CO    80215  .T.
      5  574     Nellie Deutsch   23 E. Spruce    Olathe      KS    66061  .F.
. SET PRINT OFF  (cr)
```

(b) Outputting the list on both the monitor screen and printer

Figure 5-7. Using the LIST command.

into your computer system and everything your computer system responds with will be sent to *both* the display screen and the printer.

Do not issue the SET PRINT ON command if there isn't a printer attached to your computer's system unit, as it will likely put dBASE into a "permanent" wait state (expecting to hear the missing printer signal that it's ready). Incidentally, if you are in this bind, this may be an appropriate time for you to issue the Ctrl-Alt-Del key sequence that we discussed on page 10. You either bail out here or wait forever.

Deleting Records: The DELETE, RECALL, and PACK Commands

Deleting a record permanently from a dBASE file requires two steps.

During the first step, the

DELETE

command is issued to "flag" the record to be deleted with an asterisk. At this point, the record has merely been identified as one to be deleted and it is still actively part of the file. You can restore the record, if you wish, by issuing a RECALL command.

During the second step, the

PACK

command is issued to permanently delete the record. The PACK command causes dBASE to drop all records with delete flags from the file. After a file

```
. DELETE RECORD 5  (cr)
    (1 record deleted)
. LIST  (cr)
Record#  CUSTNUM NAME             STREET          CITY       STATE ZIP    CHARGE
      1  810     John T. Smith    31 Cedarcrest   Boulder    CO    80302  .T.
      2  775     Sally Jones      725 Agua Fria   Santa Fe   NM    87501  .T.
      3  690     William Holmes   3269 Fast Lane  Santa Fe   NM    87501  .F.
      4  840     Artis Smith      2332 Alameda    Lakewood   CO    80215  .T.
      5 *574     Nellie Deutsch   23 E. Spruce    Olathe     KS    66061  .F.
. RECALL RECORD 5  (cr)
    (1 record recalled)
. LIST  (cr)
Record#  CUSTNUM NAME             STREET          CITY       STATE ZIP    CHARGE
      1  810     John T. Smith    31 Cedarcrest   Boulder    CO    80302  .T.
      2  775     Sally Jones      725 Agua Fria   Santa Fe   NM    87501  .T.
      3  690     William Holmes   3269 Fast Lane  Santa Fe   NM    87501  .F.
      4  840     Artis Smith      2332 Alameda    Lakewood   CO    80215  .T.
      5  574     Nellie Deutsch   23 E. Spruce    Olathe     KS    66061  .F.
```

(a) Deleting a record and later recalling it

```
. DELETE RECORD 5  (cr)
    (1 record deleted)
. LIST  (cr)
Record#  CUSTNUM NAME             STREET          CITY       STATE ZIP    CHARGE
      1  810     John T. Smith    31 Cedarcrest   Boulder    CO    80302  .T.
      2  775     Sally Jones      725 Agua Fria   Santa Fe   NM    87501  .T.
      3  690     William Holmes   3269 Fast Lane  Santa Fe   NM    87501  .F.
      4  840     Artis Smith      2332 Alameda    Lakewood   CO    80215  .T.
      5 *574     Nellie Deutsch   23 E. Spruce    Olathe     KS    66061  .F.
. PACK  (cr)
    (4 records copied)
. LIST  (cr)
Record#  CUSTNUM NAME             STREET          CITY       STATE ZIP    CHARGE
      1  810     John T. Smith    31 Cedarcrest   Boulder    CO    80302  .T.
      2  775     Sally Jones      725 Agua Fria   Santa Fe   NM    87501  .T.
      3  690     William Holmes   3269 Fast Lane  Santa Fe   NM    87501  .F.
      4  840     Artis Smith      2332 Alameda    Lakewood   CO    80215  .T.
```

(b) Deleting a record permanently

Figure 5-8. Using the DELETE, RECALL, and PACK commands.

has been packed, the deleted records no longer exist and cannot be recalled.

Deleting a record from the CUSTOMER file and later issuing the

RECALL

command to reinstate it is demonstrated in Figure 5-8*a*. Using the PACK command to permanently delete the record is illustrated in Figure 5-8*b*.

Editing Records: The EDIT Command

Changing data in records may be necessary for a variety of reasons. A customer may have moved, requiring a street address to be changed. Or the price of a product may have gone up. Or data originally typed into a field may have been incorrect. Whatever the case, editing allows us to change the values contained in the fields of any database records.

For example suppose customer #2, Sally Jones, has changed her Santa Fe (New Mexico) street address from "725 Agua Fria" to "Rt. 9, Box 2". Suppose also that her ZIP code has changed from 87501 to 87505. To update her record to reflect these changes issue the command

.EDIT 2 (cr)

This tells dBASE that we would like to edit record #2 (Sally's record).

At this point, you'll get a screen similar to the one in Figure 5-6*b* or 5-6*d*, depending respectively on whether you're in dBASE II or III. Hit the **Enter** key twice to move to the STREET field and type in the new street data. Then hit the **Enter** key three more times to move down to the ZIP field and enter the new ZIP code.

When you are finished, type

^W

(by depressing the **Control** key while hitting the **W** key). The **^W** (control-W) command tells dBASE that you are finished with the edit and want to save the changes. Also, it will return you to the dot prompt.

You can use the **LIST** command to check to see that the record has been edited properly.

Extracting Information: The DISPLAY Command

Up to this point, everything we've done in dBASE has involved learning how to *create* and *maintain* files. Now it's time to use dBASE as a tool for extracting valuable information from a file.

To show how this can be done, we'll enlarge the CUSTOMER file we originally started with in Figure 5-1*a*. So, complete typing the 16-record customer file shown in Figure 5-9. Since we've deleted some records along the way, and the APPEND command will only let you add records to the *end* of the file, the fastest way to proceed at this point may be to delete every remaining record beyond record #1 (John T. Smith) and start APPENDing from there.

There are many ways that we can extract data from dBASE files. We'll go through several forms of the DISPLAY command to show how you can find information quickly. Before you begin, you should **LIST** the CUSTOMER file (to see that it is exactly like the file in Figure 5-9), make sure the CUSTOMER file is open, and ascertain that the dot prompt is awaiting you on your monitor's screen.

EXAMPLE 1. **.DISPLAY ALL OFF (cr).**
This statement is similar (but not identical) to the LIST command. The keyword ALL causes all records to be displayed on the monitor screen. The keyword OFF will suppress the record numbers. A major difference between DISPLAY and LIST is that DISPLAY causes records to be displayed a screen at a time, whereas LIST causes them to be scrolled onto (and

Record #	CUSTNUM	NAME	STREET	CITY	STATE	ZIP	CHARGE
1	810	John T. Smith	31 Cedarcrest	Boulder	CO	80302	.T.
2	775	Sally Jones	725 Agua Fria	Santa Fe	NM	87501	.T.
3	690	William Holmes	3269 Fast Lane	Santa Fe	NM	87501	.F.
4	840	Artis Smith	2332 Alameda	Lakewood	CO	80215	.T.
5	574	Nellie Deutsch	23 E. Spruce	Olathe	KS	66061	.F.
6	447	Vernon Pressy	5541 Canyon	Boulder	CO	80302	.T.
7	480	Benton Fink	440 Arapahoe	Boulder	CO	80302	.F.
8	401	Wayne Montoya	600 Tara Lane	Englewood	CO	80155	.F.
9	640	C. Foster Kane	P.O. Box 6000	Santa Fe	NM	87501	.T.
10	505	Alice Evans	5702 North St.	Boise	ID	83704	.T.
11	102	Maya Ellis	603 Oakwood	Aurora	CO	80011	.T.
12	754	Shane Williams	275 East Kiowa	Flagstaff	AZ	86001	.F.
13	801	Del Lopez	80 Williston	Austin	TX	78755	.F.
14	908	Duke Miller	CM Ranch	Stanley	NM	87056	.F.
15	665	Bette White	Box 20	Rowe	NM	87562	.T.
16	760	Kim Lundy	44 West St.	Missoula	MT	59802	.F.

Figure 5-9. An expanded version of the CUSTOMER file of Figure 5-1a.

possibly off of) the screen. For long files (with DISPLAY), press any key to get the next screen of records.

EXAMPLE 2. **.DISPLAY ALL OFF CUSTNUM, NAME, CHARGE (cr).**
This form of the DISPLAY command identifies specific fields to be displayed. Thus, only the CUSTNUM, NAME, and CHARGE fields of each record will be output.

EXAMPLE 3. **.DISPLAY ALL OFF FOR STATE = "CO" (cr).**
This statement will produce a listing of all records with "CO" (Colorado) as the STATE field. The FOR clause, when used with the DISPLAY command, tells dBASE to select only those records meeting the *conditional expression* that follows the keyword FOR.

Conditional expressions in dBASE are constructed much the same way as they are in high-level programming languages such as BASIC, Pascal, COBOL, and FORTRAN. That is, they are typically formed by a field name, followed by one or more *relational operators* (such as = or >) and a constant. For example,

STATE = "NM"
CITY = "Boulder"
ZIP = 43411
PRICE < 50.00
PRICE >= 100.00
CHARGE

(Note in the above examples that the logical field name, CHARGE, implies the *logical* relation

CHARGE = "True"

and that *character* constants—such as "NM" and "Boulder"—appear in quotes.)

Compound expressions can be formed using one or more of the three connectors

.NOT.
.AND.
.OR.

If, say, we want a listing of all records representing states other than Colorado, we could execute the DISPLAY statement as

.DISPLAY ALL OFF FOR .NOT. STATE = "CO" (cr)

Or, if we wanted a listing of records representing customers from either New Mexico or Colorado, we could write

.DISPLAY ALL OFF FOR STATE = "NM" .OR. STATE = "CO" (cr)

The .OR. connector causes selection of records meeting *either* or *both* conditions. In this particular case, the way the file is set up, it's actually impossible for a person to be both from Colorado and from New Mexico. However, if we had issued a statement such as

.DISPLAY ALL OFF FOR STATE = "NM" .OR. CHARGE (cr)

it is possible to find customers who do meet one or both conditions—that is,

- They are from New Mexico but don't have a charge account.
- They are not from New Mexico, but they do have a charge account.
- They are both from New Mexico and have a charge account.

The .AND. connector is used to display records meeting *only both* of the conditions that it joins. For example, if we had entered

.DISPLAY ALL OFF FOR STATE = "NM" .AND. CHARGE (cr)

we would get only New Mexico customers with charge accounts.

There are many other forms of the DISPLAY command and forms of conditional expressions in addition to those shown here. Unfortunately, a full discussion of these is beyond the scope of this *Guide*. Before we go on, you might be interested in knowing that conditional expressions can be used with other dBASE commands, such as DELETE and LIST. For example,

.DELETE FOR STATE = "CO" (cr)

would mark all Colorado records for deletion.

Leaving dBASE: The QUIT Command

To leave dBASE and return to DOS simply invoke

.QUIT (cr)

OTHER USEFUL dBASE OPERATIONS

There are many other dBASE facilities that probably would be useful to you in addition to those discussed so far. Here we'll discuss three more: sorting data, relating two files, and preparing a report from a file.

Sorting Data

Let's return to the 16-record CUSTOMER file of Figure 5-9. You'll now learn how to sort data from this file.

In dBASE, as well as many other data management software packages, sorting is most efficiently done through a procedure called *indexing.* To do this we first identify a *key field* on which we want to sort records. For example, say we want a listing of the CUSTOMER file, in ascending order by customer number. Hence CUSTNUM would be our key field.

Next we must issue a special dBASE command that will produce an *index file* of CUSTOMER with respect to the CUSTNUM field. The index file determines the order in which CUSTOMER's records would appear if CUSTOMER were to be sorted by the CUSTNUM field. Note that the CUSTOMER file itself is never sorted and will remain unaltered in the process. The index file we'll ask dBASE to create for CUSTOMER will look something like the file in Figure 5-10. Note that if we output the records of CUSTOMER in the order suggested by this index file (customer 102, customer 401, and so on) the records will be in the proper sorted sequence.

Let's now create the index file we've just described. First, make sure you've issued the proper USE command to get dBASE to point to CUSTOMER. Then enter

.INDEX ON CUSTNUM TO NUMINDX (cr)

This command creates, on the B-drive disk, an index file for CUSTOMER called

NUMINDX.NDX

All index files stored by dBASE have the extension .NDX.* However, because you'll be using these files in restricted contexts, where dBASE can identify them, you will not be explicity declaring this extension when in dBASE.

This particular index file is keyed into CUSTOMER's CUSTNUM

*Because index files have a different extension (NDX) than that (DBF) of the files they index, both of these files can have the same name.

Indexing Order	Record #	CUSTNUM
1	11	102
2	8	401
3	6	447
4	7	480
5	10	505
6	5	574
7	9	640
8	15	665
9	3	690
10	12	754
11	16	760
12	2	775
13	13	801
14	1	810
15	4	840
16	14	908

Figure 5-10. An index file for the CUSTOMER file. The key field, CUSTNUM, is arranged low to high.

field. If we want a sorted listing of the records in CUSTOMER, we now issue the command

.SET INDEX TO NUMINDX (cr)

This tells dBASE to open the NUMINDX index file. Just as .DBF files must be opened with the USE command, .NDX files are not usable unless they are first opened.

Next, to list the records in sorted order, simply type

.LIST (cr)

The sequence of operator instructions—and dBASE actions—that we've just described are shown in Figure 5-11.

It's also possible in dBASE to index a file in descending order on the key field. If the key field is numeric, this is rather straightforward—you simply put a minus character ("–") before the name of the key field in the INDEX statement. If the key field is character, a more complicated procedure (beyond the scope of the *Guide*) must be followed. Also, the procedure to follow depends on whether you are using dBASE II or dBASE III. If you are a beginner needing to do a descending sort, either make the key field numeric at the outset (if that's possible) or use the SORT command (discussed shortly).

We can create *several* index files for any file with a .DBF extension. For example, the following statements show an index file being created for the

```
. USE CUSTOMER  (cr)
. INDEX ON CUSTNUM TO NUMINDX  (cr)
    (16 records indexed)
. SET INDEX TO NUMINDX  (cr)
. LIST  (cr)


Record#  CUSTNUM NAME             STREET           CITY         STATE ZIP    CHARGE
    11   102     Maya Ellis       603 Oakwood      Aurora       CO    80011  .T.
     8   401     Wayne Montoya    600 Tara Lane    Englewood    CO    80155  .F.
     6   447     Vernon Pressy    5541 Canyon      Boulder      CO    80302  .T.
     7   480     Benton Fink      440 Arapahoe     Boulder      CO    80302  .F.
    10   505     Alice Evans      5702 North St.   Boise        ID    83704  .T.
     5   574     Nellie Deutsch   23 E. Spruce     Olathe       KS    66061  .F.
     9   640     C. Foster Kane   P.O. Box 6000    Santa Fe     NM    87501  .T.
    15   665     Bette White      Box 20           Rowe         NM    87562  .T.
     3   690     William Holmes   3269 Fast Lane   Santa Fe     NM    87501  .F.
    12   754     Shane Williams   275 East Kiowa   Flagstaff    AZ    86001  .F.
    16   760     Kim Lundy        44 West St.      Missoula     MT    59802  .F.
     2   775     Sally Jones      725 Aqua Fria    Santa Fe     NM    87501  .T.
    13   801     Del Lopez        80 Williston     Austin       TX    78755  .F.
     1   810     John T. Smith    31 Cedarcrest    Boulder      CO    80302  .T.
     4   840     Artis Smith      2332 Alameda     Lakewood     CO    80215  .T.
    14   908     Duke Miller      CM Ranch         Stanley      NM    87056  .F.
```

Figure 5-11. Sorting the CUSTOMER file by customer number.

ZIP code field of CUSTOMER and, also, this index file (ZIPINDX) being used with CUSTOMER to arrange records by ZIP code.

.USE CUSTOMER (cr)
.INDEX ON ZIP TO ZIPINDX (cr)
.SET INDEX TO ZIPINDX (cr)
.LIST (cr)

And, finally, we can also index a file on *multiple* key fields. For example, if we wanted a listing of customers that was arranged first by ZIP code and then, within ZIP codes, by customer number, we would issue the series of statements below:

.USE CUSTOMER (cr)
.INDEX ON ZIP + CUSTNUM TO DBLINDX (cr)
.SET INDEX TO DBLINDX (cr)
.LIST (cr)

dBASE also has a regular **SORT** command that, although conceptually more straightforward than indexing, is far less computationally efficient. Using SORT creates a new DBF file, unlike using INDEX, and thus uses much more memory.

Relating Two Files

The power of database technology is fully realized when we relate data that exists in two or more files. In dBASE one way this is done is through the JOIN command. The JOIN command enables us to combine data from two files to form a third file. Here we'll go through a simple example to show you how to join data from the CUSTOMER and ORDER files of Figure 5-1.

What we wish to do is produce, on the display screen, the file shown in Figure 5-12*a*. Note that preparing this file requires linking data in the ORDER file (order numbers and dates) with data in the CUSTOMER file (customer names, cities, and states). ORDER and CUSTOMER are related, so to speak, by their common field—customer number (CUSTNUM)—as you can see by referring to Figure 5-1. When two files are joined, they are not altered.

```
ORDNUM DATE      NAME              CITY       STATE
003     2/7/87   John T. Smith     Boulder    CO
005     2/16/87  John T. Smith     Boulder    CO
006     2/18/87  John T. Smith     Boulder    CO
001     2/3/87   Sally Jones       Santa Fe   NM
002     2/5/87   Sally Jones       Santa Fe   NM
004     2/16/87  Nellie Deutsch    Olathe     KS
```

(a) Output from JOIN

```
. SELECT SECONDARY  (cr)
. USE ORDER  (cr)
. SELECT PRIMARY  (cr)
. USE CUSTOMER  (cr)
. JOIN WITHORDER  TO ORDCUST ;   (cr)
     FOR CUSTNUM = S.CUSTNUM ;   (cr)
     FIELDS ORDNUM, DATE, NAME, CITY, STATE  (cr)
. USE ORDCUST  (cr)
. DISPLAY ALL OFF  (cr)
```

(b) dBASE II commands

```
. SELECT 2  (cr)
. USE ORDER ALIAS SMITH  (cr)
. SELECT 1  (cr)
. USE CUSTOMER  (cr)
. JOIN WITH SMITH TO ORDCUST ;   (cr)
     FOR CUSTNUM = SMITH->CUSTNUM ;   (cr)
     FIELDS ORDNUM, DATE, NAME, CITY, STATE  (cr)
. USE ORDCUST  (cr)
. DISPLAY ALL OFF  (cr)
```

(c) dBASE III commands

Figure 5-12. Relating two files with the JOIN command.

The series of dBASE statements that we would have to enter to produce the information we require is shown for dBASE II users in Figure 5-12*b*, and for dBASE III users in Figure 5-12*c*. The SELECT command enables us to keep two or more files active at the same time. In both dBASE II and III the purpose of SELECT is to establish separate work areas for each of the active files.

The USE command that follows each SELECT command stores the file that's just been SELECTed in the designated work area. Remember, the USE command also points to a file. Although we can have several files active at the same time, the last-issued USE command before the JOIN command names the file that will be designated as the *currently selected file* for joining purposes. This is significant because the JOIN command does not explicitly name the currently selected file but refers to it implicitly.

You should also note that the syntax of the SELECT command is not identical in dBASE II and III. In dBASE II, a maximum of two work areas can be established. These are referred to as the PRIMARY and SECONDARY work areas. dBASE III allows for 10 active work areas, numbered 1 to 10. The primary work area is referred to by the number 1; the secondary work area, by the number 2; and so on.

The syntax of dBASE III's the JOIN command is provided below:

```
.JOIN WITH filename-X TO filename-Y ;
        FOR condition(s) ;
        [FIELDS fieldname list]
```

Note that the currently selected filename is never named in the command. We are pointing to it. Filename-X refers to the file that is *not* currently selected. Filename-Y refers to the new file that will result from the JOIN. In dBASE II the JOIN command has no WITH clause.

All capitalized words in the syntax shown are *keywords* and (except for FIELDS) must be present in every JOIN statement. The square brackets around the FIELDS clause indicates that it is *optional*—that is, you don't need the FIELDS clause if the new file created from the JOIN will contain all fields from both the primary and secondary files. However, if you are extracting only certain fields from these files (as in the example shown in Figure 5-12) this clause must be present. The semicolons at the end the first two lines tell dBASE that the rest of the JOIN statement follows. Also, there must be a blank space before each semicolon.

dBASE III requires users to declare an *alias* name, of up to 10 characters, for filename-X. This alias name is used to identify this file after the keyword WITH in the JOIN statement, and also in the FOR clause—where it is combined with a 2-character pointing device made up of the hyphen character (-) and the greater-than symbol (>). The FOR clause attempts to relate the primary and secondary files through their common field—CUSTNUM. Since this field appears in both files, dBASE requires us to use the pointing mechanism shown whenever we are making reference to CUSTNUM in the file that is *not* currently selected. Thus, what the FOR clause is actually saying is "FOR all occurrences where CUSTNUM in the currently selected file can be matched with CUSTNUM in the not currently selected file."

dBASE II does not use an aliasing system. Instead, the qualifier P. is used in front of a field name if it is from the primary file and the primary file is not currently selected. Similarly, the qualifier S. is used in front of the field name if it is from the secondary file and the secondary file is not currently selected. Field names from currently selected files do not need qualifiers.

Creating Reports

Although there is not sufficient space to adequately discuss this topic here, you should know that dBASE has a powerful feature to enable you to prepare reports, such as the invoice in Figure 5-3. dBASE will allow you to format the report to your needs, calculate columns of numbers where appropriate, request subtotals and totals at certain junctures of the report, date the report, and so forth.

The procedures that you must follow to implement the *report generator feature* in dBASE II and dBASE III differ considerably. Both packages require you to first define the "structure" of the report in a *report form,* a disk file that describes to dBASE how the report will be prepared. However, dBASE II and III use a different command to invoke the report form, and the procedures to prepare the form are not the same.

If you want to learn how to prepare reports in your dBASE package, consult an appropriate dBASE trade book or go to the appropriate dBASE reference manual. Look for commands that use the keyword REPORT.

Exercises

1. Log into dBASE. Using the PRODUCT file in Figure 5-1*b*
   - **a.** Create a structure for this file with the CREATE command. Use a field width of 3 characters for the product number and 25 characters for the product description. Define the PRICE field so that it can accommodate a price as large as $999.99.
   - **b.** Open the file with the USE command and enter records into it with the APPEND command.
   - **c.** Display the contents of the file on your monitor screen with the LIST command. Also, if there is a printer attached to your computer system, output the records on the printer.
   - **d.** Using the DELETE command, mark (with an asterisk) the following records for deletion:

     002 Nylon Windpants
     005 Rozelle Headband

e. RECALL the records deleted in step d.

f. Using both the DELETE and PACK commands, permanently delete the records referred to in step d.

g. Using the EDIT command, change the price of the Nordic Hat to $15.00 and the price of the Thermal Ski Socks to $8.00

h. Use the APPEND command to add the following records to the file:

006	Work Gloves	15.00
007	Pocket Tool	50.00
008	Yuppie Polar Sunglasses	75.00
009	Sheepskin Seat Covers	150.00

i. Using the DISPLAY command, extract records pertaining to items costing at least $50.00. (*Hint:* Write the associated condition as PRICE >= 50.00.)

j. QUIT dBASE and go back to DOS.

2. Using the data originally shown in the PRODUCT file of Figure 5-1*b*, sort this file in alphabetical order, using DESCRIP as the key field.

3. Create a database of 15–30 students, using the following field suggestions:

- ID Number (3 characters)
- Name (20 characters, e.g., Johnson, Linda)
- Major (3 characters, e.g., ACC for accounting)
- Home State (2 characters, e.g., CA for California)
- Year in School (1 character, e.g., 1 for freshman, 2 for sophomore, etc.)
- Scholarship Status (1 character, e.g. T for scholarship, F for no scholarship)

Define the database structure so that all fields are *character* except for Year in School (which is *numeric*) and Scholarship Status (which is *logical*). Design records for the file so that about 5 to 6 different majors are represented, about half of the students are in-state (with about 3 to 4 other states represented), and students in each year of school are represented.

Once you've set up the database, use it to DISPLAY information such as the following:

a. The names of all seniors

b. The names of all in-state seniors

c. The names of all students who are *either* seniors or in-state

d. The names of all students who are beyond the freshman year

e. The names of all students, sorted first by year (i.e., freshman first, then sophomores, etc.); then, sorted alphabetically by name

f. The names of all in-state accounting majors who are on scholarship

Index